The Simple Yet Effective Methods to Cure Procrastination

Blueprint to Solving the Time Management Puzzle and Develop Habits Boosting Your Productivity with Over 7 Concise Strategies

Werner K. Clark

© Copyright 2019 - All rights reserved.

The content contained within this book may not be reproduced, duplicated or transmitted without direct written permission from the author or the publisher.

Under no circumstances will any blame or legal responsibility be held against the publisher, or author, for any damages, reparation, or monetary loss due to the information contained within this book. Either directly or indirectly.

Legal Notice:

This book is copyright protected. This book is only for personal use. You cannot amend, distribute, sell, use, quote or paraphrase any part, or the content within this book, without the consent of the author or publisher.

Disclaimer Notice:

Please note the information contained within this document is for educational and entertainment purposes only. All effort has been executed to present accurate, up to date, and reliable, complete information. No warranties of any kind are declared or implied. Readers acknowledge that the author is not engaging in the rendering of legal, financial, medical or professional advice. The content within this book has been derived from various sources. Please consult a licensed professional before attempting any techniques outlined in this book.

By reading this document, the reader agrees that under no circumstances is the author responsible for any losses, direct or indirect, which are incurred as a result of the use of information contained within this document, including, but not limited to, — errors, omissions, or inaccuracies.

Contents

Chapter 1:
The Science Behind Why You Procrastinate _____ 1

Chapter 2:
5 Steps to Stop Procrastinating _____ 14

Chapter 3:
How to Stop Wasting Time _____ 25

Chapter 4:
Get Organized and Productive Even with a Hectic Schedule _____ 41

Chapter 5:
The Secret to Become Motivated _____ 57

Chapter 6:
Guaranteed Tricks to Make Habits Stick _____ 71

Chapter 7:
The 5 Non-Obvious Things That Kill Your Productivity _____ 83

Chapter 8:
How to Set REAL Goals You Will Stick To _____ 92

Chapter 9:
How to Stop Being Tired All the Time _____ 100

Chapter 10:
The Secret to Work with Intense Focus _____ 114

Chapter 11:
Essential Apps that FORCE You to Be More Productive _____ 119

Chapter 12:
Wake Up Motivated Every Day Hack _____ 134

My Final Words_____ 136

Chapter 1:
The Science Behind Why You Procrastinate

Procrastination is you delaying or avoiding doing a task that has vital importance. It is common in most humans. It may be noticeable in some instances and difficult to identify in others.

Procrastination and Laziness

A common error that people make is to confuse procrastination for laziness. These are two different concepts. To procrastinate, an individual will opt for a task that appears to be easy, less strenuous, and less urgent in favor of more pressing work that seems to be difficult. You are postponing a task to do another task that is more pleasurable but usually has less significance. Laziness, on the other hand, is the act of remaining idle instead of performing a task. In this case, you don't carry out any other task during the time but choose to be inactive for that period. There is no motivation to do the work at hand, but you motivate yourself to avoid putting the effort required. A significant similarity between a procrastinator and a lazy individual is the lack of motivation to perform a task. The huge difference, in this case, is that while the lazy individual has no apparent intention of completing the task in question, a procrastinator will finish it later.

Why Do We Procrastinate?

As an individual, you must have had a reason to procrastinate at one time or the other. Although it is more noticeable in some individuals, it is often negligible in others. It is easy to remember certain cases where you have put things off just because you felt you had enough time. You may also not forget other instances in which you were looking for the best way to start a project, so you had to delay.

Most people tend to underestimate the work and effort required to complete a task. As a result, they wait until the last minute to complete the task. The wait for the 'right time' or proper motivation to perform a task also plays a role. There are lots of reasons why people procrastinate. Understanding the reason why you procrastinate is often the first step to eliminating procrastination. Below are some of the prominent reasons why procrastinators do what they do:

No Sense of Urgency in The Task

Most of the time, it is easier to pay attention to a task that appears to be urgent. It is the same principle we apply when prioritizing activities for the day.

There are things that we don't create time to do just because it doesn't seem urgent now. Although it may be on your To-Do list for months or years, you may never create time to complete these tasks.

The Simple Yet Effective Methods to Cure Procrastination

It is easier to feed a crying baby than it is to visit a cousin in another State.

You Don't Know Where to Start

How do I start? What is the first step to take? These are questions that often lead to procrastination. It is easy to get confused, become disorganized, or feel overwhelmed when you are unsure of the first step to take. When this feeling comes into play, it becomes difficult to get yourself to do a task. It is a unique type of procrastination which is caused by negative emotions and not avoidance. Negative emotions often result in feelings of incompetence. An individual will prefer to play a video game instead of attempting a task that makes them develop feelings of self-doubt.

You Have A Fear of Failure

As individuals, we often set high-standards that we need to match when performing a task. In other cases, these standards are put in place by society. The fear of receiving harsh judgment due to a task you complete can lead to procrastination. If you think you won't be able to meet the societal standards or those you have set, it becomes easy to put off work. If you don't do anything, no-one will judge you. It is an easy escape from what you fear the most. Through this act, you eliminate the option of failing. It is a method that works for as long as you can delay.

An individual that has a fear of failure will find comfort in procrastination. If given the opportunity to make a choice, people will pick a subjective failure over actual failure. Subjective failure implies that you fail at a task since you don't perform the task. Actual failure suggests that you put effort into the task but produced undesirable results.

The Excuse of Working Better Under Pressure

Sometimes it is easier to refer to this as crisis-making. It is a situation where an individual believes that they do their best work when there is a lot of pressure on them. Have you ever gone over an entire course outline two days to the exam? If you achieve success, in this case, it is easy to believe that you can work under pressure. You often love the adrenaline rush that comes with the pressure. It is also a way for you to escape the boredom you are feeling.

You Don't Want to Do Your Work

There are specific tasks that you don't want to do. It is much more fun to play video games than to do the dishes or arrange your room. If the tasks before you are boring, an opportunity for a more enjoyable task is the obvious choice. Once a task makes you feel bored, it becomes difficult to do it.

Distractions

Sometimes, you may be willing to complete the task at hand. The main problem is you get distracted very easily. It means you always find something that seems better than the task at hand. Distractions often result in instant gratification. Completing a task will usually result in satisfaction, but it takes more time. There are lots of activities that serve as distractions. To some individuals, it may be access to the internet or social media sites. To other individuals, it may be video games. It is common for people to have multiple distractions.

You Worry Too Much

When you worry too much, it becomes difficult to achieve anything. You become anxious due to worry. Things often appear to carry excess risk to an individual that worries. It may also seem like an unnecessary task. As a result, they prefer to avoid putting up with the challenges that come with the task. Worrying often results in self-doubt. It develops the feeling of incompetence. To avoid self-doubt and incompetence, it is usually more palatable to remain in a position where you are comfortable.

The Need for Perfection

A large percentage of procrastinators are perfectionists. It means that they want a task to be perfect on completion. It often results in delays. As a perfectionist, the goals you set for a task can be unrealistic and overwhelming. Completing the task then becomes very difficult since what you hope to achieve is seemingly impossible. Trying to get time to put in the right details will often lead to procrastination.

Low Energy

Your energy level usually determines how much work you get done. A low energy level implies that you will be unable to do much. It indirectly leads to procrastination.

A low energy level is common in individuals that have an unhealthy lifestyle. It may be a poor diet or low quality of sleep that results in sluggishness or tiredness. The cause of low energy levels will differ for every individual so learning your reason for low energy is essential. To provide the necessary energy boost for a day, a lot of people perform exercises. Individuals that perform exercises in the morning will be motivated for work during the day through the energy boost it provides. Recognizing that you have a low energy level is quite easy. It may show a lack of physical energy to perform important tasks. You often find it easier to sit on a couch and watch television.

Finding Reasons to Delay
Delaying means you are simply putting off various tasks for certain reasons. The delay of a task is often not dependent on its urgency or difficulty in this case. Sometimes the reasons may be valid while at other times they may not. Some of these reasons include business and fatigue. When an individual claim to be busy, it may be a valid reason. Nonetheless, business may often result from an inability to say no when necessary. As a result, you receive so many tasks that it becomes overwhelming. Fatigue may also result from having too much to do.

Creating Too Many Lists

Making lists is a meaningful way to organize your tasks as well as your thoughts. So, what happens when you make excessive lists? Too many lists often result in too many things to consider. You pay attention to the smallest details of a project. In most cases, you are unable to get any actual work done during the time you spend creating a comprehensive list.

You Lack Vision

In some cases, individuals often procrastinate when they have no idea of the end goal behind a task or its importance. The absence of a bigger picture commonly causes procrastination. The bigger picture is often the end goal or the vision of a project. A vision is a guide to a long-term goal. Without a guide, it is much more reasonable to focus on the things that will have an impact on the present. Through an excellent vision, it is easy to act towards a goal.

Acting in Defiance Toward Authority

There are times when things may seem to be unfair in a work environment. It may be a simple situation where you are given more tasks than your colleagues. It can also be due to being under the supervision of someone you don't get along with. In a bid to prove your individuality, it is easy to postpone tasks given in such situations. It may simply be to prove a point. As a result, you end up procrastinating simply because the task is from a person that you don't respect.

How Does Procrastination Negatively Impact You?

Procrastination affects individuals in more ways than they are willing to admit. It is noticeable when procrastination becomes the lifestyle of an individual. A chronic procrastinator will often get a fine due to late tax payments. It is also common for others to do their share of a project at work to avoid missing deadlines. It is also common to notice higher stress levels in procrastinators since they end up doing a large portion of work in a very short time.

Social relationship is another aspect of life that is negatively impacted by procrastination. A lot of people stop depending on you because you consistently let them down. You may fail at a relationship because you have a habit of changing plans at the last minute. There are other negative effects of procrastination in life. Below, you will find some of the impacts which are steadily dragging you backward in life:

You Miss Important Opportunities

Opportunities in life often come and go. How you handle these opportunities when they come your way is important. Do you take opportunities as soon as they open? Or do you assume it will be available until you are ready? Opportunities are often once-in-a-lifetime events. If you miss it the first time, there is no guarantee of a second time. For this reason, you need to take immediate action when they arrive.

The Simple Yet Effective Methods to Cure Procrastination

Procrastination will often prevent you from making that split-second decision that would have changed your life for the better. It could be an opening for a scholarship. You may fail to grab this opportunity if you procrastinate on writing an application for the scholarship. Scholarships usually have a closing date for applications with conditions that may make it impossible to apply due to age restrictions.

It Lowers Your Self-Esteem

Low-self-esteem is a leading cause of procrastination in most individuals. Also, procrastination also lowers your self-esteem. It means that there is a cycle that keeps on going when you procrastinate. By keeping the cycle going, you are not only missing opportunities and ruining your career – you are also steadily destroying yourself.

Various self-destructive tendencies result from low self-esteem. It becomes easy to doubt yourself, and you also believe that you don't deserve certain achievements. You hold yourself from taking a step towards progress, and then the frequent question becomes, "Why can't I just take a step forward?" Although it happens slowly over a period, procrastination feeds on your confidence.

Inability to Meet Your Goals

The things you set out to achieve or those you intend to change usually develop into your goals. It is easy to motivate yourself when coming up with the goals you want to meet.

Procrastination will often prevent you from meeting these goals. It may lead to a delay in acting or taking the first step towards the goal. It can easily overshadow your strong desire to make these changes or achieve something new. You may think to yourself, "I want it so bad so I will get it." Procrastination is a stronger resistance. Goals often turn our lives around for the better. The inability to achieve these goals means that there will be no noticeable progress in life.

Health Challenges

Anxiety and stress are some of the mental health challenges that have a close relationship with procrastination. Depression may often result from actions of procrastination. As time goes by, other areas of your life will be affected by the negative impact of depression. The anxiety and stress are often the results of procrastinating on a task excessively. It becomes visible if there are other individuals involved in the task.

Delaying or postponing your visit or appointment with the doctor or dentist is a much clearer picture of how procrastination affects your health. You may also postpone exercises that are meant to get your body in proper shape. In both cases, the effect of procrastination can be a lot worse than what you imagine.

You Could Put Your Career in Jeopardy

When building your career, your achievements, results, and how your work has a direct effect on your growth. There are various ways procrastination can affect this growth. Procrastination may result in an inability to meet your monthly targets while also affecting your ability to meet deadlines.

If you consistently miss deadlines or monthly targets, you may lose clients and miss opportunities for promotions. The worst-case scenario is that you will be out of the job in a short time. Short-term procrastination may be easy to cover up. Long-term procrastination will expose you to ruin. It is often a common cause of crashes on the path to career growth.

You Waste Valuable Time

Procrastination is often a time-wasting activity. It is more noticeable when you procrastinate on a task that has a direct influence on your life.

Determining the time, you waste procrastinating is not as easy as it sounds. Nonetheless, it is easy to notice that it has been three years after graduation without any step towards progress in your career. Now you start thinking about how you didn't apply for any professional course or add a new qualification to your CV during these years. In some cases, it may be failing to put in the necessary effort to pass a course. When you fail at an educational course, you often must wait until the next year to have a second chance.

Since you can't go back in time to make the necessary changes, you are left with regrets that are often very terrible feelings. Regrets appear when you start thinking about how you could have done things differently, how you could have tried, or how you shouldn't have given up. Depending on how important the task is to your life, you may have to create more time to achieve the goal.

Poor Decision-Making

Procrastinating on important tasks is one thing but making decisions while doing this always has a negative impact. The decisions you make will always be poor. But how does procrastination affect my decision making?

It is simple. Procrastination creates a new set of conditions that will not be present if you already completed a task. Making decisions based on the new conditions will often lead to poor decisions. One such condition is the pressure that builds up when your deadline is getting close. You begin to make hasty decisions without thinking them through. Emotions like, "How you would feel bad if you are labeled incompetent" also start to creep into your decision-making process. The results you produce in life often depend on the decisions you make, either good decisions or poor decisions.

It Has a Negative Influence on Your Reputation

If you keep making promises you can't keep, no-one will be willing to work with you. It means that you have a reputation for letting people down. It is one of the effects of procrastination.

The Simple Yet Effective Methods to Cure Procrastination

It happens when you promise to help others with a task and fail to deliver on the promise by the deadline. As soon as you understand that you already have a reputation for missing deadlines, you also make it easy to procrastinate. No-one is surprised by your behavior, and neither are you. One of the problems that come with a damaged reputation includes the unwillingness of other people to depend on you. It can result in missed opportunities down the line. Your friends and co-workers don't want to be stuck cleaning up your mess after you fail to deliver.

Chapter 2:
5 Steps to Stop Procrastinating

Stopping procrastination will be impossible if you don't take any action. In acting, the right move is also significant. In this chapter, I will be discussing the best steps to take in stopping procrastination.

Forgive Yourself for Procrastinating
The infusion of negative emotions into your life is much easier when you engage in self-criticism. It generates emotions like depression, fear of failure, and anxiety. These are emotions that distract you from your goals, prevent you from taking actions, and disrupt your focus. You cannot create an environment that promotes your best performance through self-criticism. Failure is often a good way to learn your weaknesses and improve on them. If you don't take any action, you don't have the opportunity to fail or learn from your failures.

Why You Should Forgive Yourself
When you can forgive yourself for your failure, it becomes easy to go after a new goal quickly. You are more focused on growth and avoid dwelling on the past. Your desire to grow and learn outweighs your focus on performance-based goals. Since you don't have a fear of

failure, you are less likely to take actions that result in procrastination. It becomes easier to create plans that will lead you towards a specific goal.

Another significant benefit of forgiving yourself is the improvement in health. You are less prone to depression, anxiety, or stress. It will also follow through on health-related goals like weight-loss. Admitting mistakes, recognizing parts of your life that need enhancement, and being accountable for your actions is also possible if you can forgive yourself. Forgiving yourself when you procrastinate is a three-step process. It includes the following steps:

- Understanding and accepting that you are procrastinating. Allowing your body experience regrets, guilt, and the feelings that follow.

- Forgiving yourself for these feelings.

Understanding and Accepting That You Are Procrastinating

Sometimes, shifting a task to a later time may not be procrastination. In such situations, there is usually a legitimate reason why this task must be done later. It is what we refer to as re-prioritizing.

When you start evading tasks for an indefinite period without any genuine reason, then you are probably procrastinating. There are other signs of procrastination you should look out for. These include the following:

- Having a recurring item with significant importance on your To-Do list without taking any action.

- Stopping mid-way through a high-priority task to get a cup of coffee or respond to social media messages.

- Having a schedule filled with tasks of low-priority.

- Delaying until the 'right time' or 'right mood' to start a task. Failure to make decisions despite going through your emails over and over.

- Delaying your high-priority tasks while completing low-priority tasks that other people have assigned to you.

Experiencing Regrets and Guilt

The only way you will have the opportunity to forgive yourself is by experiencing certain negative emotions. If you fail to meet a deadline as a result of procrastination, it may often lead to self-criticism. It means you feel guilty for missing the deadline.

The first step is to understand that feelings of self-criticism are a natural response that is acceptable. As a human being, it is part of you. It is the same way a lot of your friends or colleagues experience fear, sadness, and anger. Negative emotions are like the rough times and difficulties in life; they will always be present. At one point, they will have to leave. It is crucial you don't judge yourself during the period these emotions are present.

Forgiving Yourself for These Feelings

The temptation to criticize your actions will always creep up. It is crucial you are vigilant any time these temptations become strong. Instead of throwing yourself under the bus, respond to these negative emotions in a more positive, compassionate manner. The secret to forgiving yourself is to recognize when you are harboring feelings of suffering, failure, and sorrow. Responding with kindness and positivity will complete the process of forgiveness.

Having a Game Plan for Achieving Goals

How you go about creating your goals can often be a reason why you procrastinate. A lot of goals we set are often as a result of our excitement at that time. Once the target is set, you have no direction, so you move towards a less stressful path. That is not how goals work. Heading in any direction that seems the best will often leave you feeling lost with thoughts that you will never reach your goal. At this point, procrastination sets in. You start making excuses like, "It is too difficult," or "I'll try again next week."

There is no way you will achieve a goal on your To-Do list without making attempts. Waiting for the best to happen without putting in the work is why a lot of people are still over-weight and why others have still not started their business. To achieve your goals, you must be ready to self-manage these goals. It is a process that involves you getting in the driver's seat and steering yourself to the best position to achieve the goal.

Developing the Plan

A goal planner is vital if you are to make any real attempt at achieving your goals. A plan is a momentum that keeps throwing you towards the goal you intend to accomplish. Your plan should include the steps that you will take from the moment you set your mind on the goal until the moment you achieve the goal. A good plan will make it difficult to procrastinate. You will only procrastinate if you don't know how to get to the next point.

Your goal planner should also include a schedule. The schedule should show a specific date when you will take the first step towards your goal. Since you have listed steps, these are small tasks within the overall project. It means that each step should have a date and a deadline. To complete each step, you must commit to the step. As you progress through each step, there should be a milestone. The milestone is a point where you will celebrate your progress so far. It is also a form of motivation that eliminates any feeling of procrastination. The momentum you gain from the small steps you complete is usually the motivation that drives you to the end of the goal.

Reviewing Regularly

The Simple Yet Effective Methods to Cure Procrastination

You can't learn a lot in life if all your focus is solely on what lies ahead. Sometimes, you need to look at how you got to your current position. It is also a way of checking for any other opportunity that is available. You can also improve your plan or re-evaluate some of the strategies within the plan. It is also a time when you re-evaluate yourself to determine if you still have the same strong feelings for the goal.

Through a review process, you will be able to identify achievements that are worth celebrating and failures that can teach you something new. You can also look at the future and the strategies for the future. Has there been any change in your circumstances to render these strategies obsolete? If a strategy is obsolete and you are unable to make changes in time, you will end up getting stuck at that point. This is when it becomes effortless to procrastinate. Your thoughts may run towards, "I've gotten quite far. I can take some time off to fix this strategy."

You also need to reflect deeply on your desires. It is acceptable for your desires towards the goal to change as your circumstances also change. The primary purpose of a review and reflection is to determine where you stand. It is also helpful in making sure you can adjust to changes in the direction that leads to your goal.

Avoid Perfectionism

Perfectionism is an unrealistic ideal that usually promotes failure and procrastination. Unrealistic expectations and perfectionism can overwhelm us and set us up for failure. When you try to be perfect, you are likely going to develop feelings of anxiousness. It may sometimes prevent you from doing the task. Finding a way to avoid perfectionism is an excellent solution to the problem of procrastination. Perfectionism is noticeable in various instances. If your thoughts are filled with phrases like, "I need this project to be perfect" or, "I don't have the right tools to do justice to this project," then you are a perfectionist.

Imagine a task where you must design a logo. If you have an unrealistic expectation of your design skills, you may worry about creating a logo that isn't perfect. It will lead you to avoid making any attempt at designing the logo. Procrastination then comes as an option to prevent coming to terms with the fact that your design isn't perfect.

Your Right to Imperfection

If you accept that you can be imperfect, then you will be able to get around to doing any task without procrastination. No-one will be able to see if you are a great logo designer if you don't design any logos. It is why you need to understand that completing a task is much better than being perfect.

Perfectionism doesn't apply to everyone. Regardless, a lot of people also procrastinate because they don't want to be judged as incompetent by others. If you find yourself in this situation often, then you there are certain steps you can take.

Simple Steps to Avoid Perfectionism

Step 1
Get a clear understanding of why you are delaying a task. Do you have unrealistic expectations for your skills?

Step 2
Come to terms with the fact that your quest for perfection is preventing you from moving forward. Recall all the instances that perfection caused you to fail at a project.

Step 3
Accept that it is okay to be imperfect. Realize that it is better to be done with a task than to seek perfection and not make any progress. There will always be opportunities to improve on a project once it is complete.

Step 4
When you are procrastinating, take note of your thoughts. Are you having perfectionist thoughts? Counter these thoughts with logical reasoning.

Break Down a Project into Small Tasks and Remove Distractions

A Smaller Task Is More Straightforward to Tackle

If you find a task overwhelming, it becomes easier to procrastinate. Dividing your larger tasks into smaller bits is a helpful way to simplify the task. Once you separate it into these smaller bits, it becomes possible to focus on each bit. If a task still looks overwhelming after breaking it down, you can simplify it further. Breaking down a task into its simplest form will make it possible to finish a small part within a short time. As you complete the smaller portions, you can make rapid progress towards the finished project.

Let your focus be on each small task so you can produce the best results. As soon as you complete a small part, you can go on to the next part. Having deadlines for each small task is equally important. A single deadline for a project can often cause individuals to procrastinate until there is no time left. Creating specific deadlines also helps when breaking down a larger task.

Since your project will have an overall deadline, you can use this as a guide when creating specific deadlines for your smaller tasks. There should be a sense of urgency when creating deadlines. In this way, you will understand that you can ruin your plans if you fail to meet any deadline.

Removing Distractions

Sometimes, we procrastinate because we run out of energy for useful work. What is the easiest way to run out of energy in the workplace? It is by having to resist distractions around you. Imagine how difficult it is to resist visiting your Facebook page if it is open in a browser tab with notifications coming in. It may be easy at first, but you are likely going to give in later. As you start scrolling through your timeline, you end up procrastinating on important tasks. You will procrastinate more if you take actions that make procrastination seem like an easy option. Using site-blocking apps can help to block any site that can be a potential distraction. It is an option that is more suitable than deleting your profile entirely.

Have Someone Hold You Accountable

Move with People That Inspire You

Being around certain individuals can influence the way you behave. If you are lucky to spend some time with Elon Musk, you are going to have the inspiration to work harder. You won't get that opportunity as frequently as you require.

Nonetheless, this simple strategy remains effective. There are lots of hard workers and go-getters that you will interact with daily. These individuals can be your colleagues at work or your friends. Spending more time with these individuals will have a positive effect on you. It becomes easy to adopt the spirit and drive they put into all their activities.

Form A Team with A Close Friend

A close friend or companion to work with makes the work process easy to cope with and fun. Any person you choose as your buddy should also have goals that he/she is looking to achieve. Each person will be answerable for their actions as regards these goals. Although it is a lot better if you and your buddy have the same goals, it is not a necessity.

Goals that are similar make it possible to learn from one another. On a much larger scale, you can also inform more friends, acquaintances, and colleagues about new projects you are working on. People will like to talk about these projects to learn about new developments.

Is There Anyone That Has Accomplished a Similar Goal?

Do you have a goal? What is the goal you want to achieve? Do you know anyone that has reached a similar goal? Connecting with people who have achieved a similar goal is very helpful. They serve as proof that the goal in your sight is achievable. It is the most suitable trigger to get you to act towards the goal.

Chapter 3:
How to Stop Wasting Time

Time-wasting is often due to the irrelevant actions that we take. A great example of an irrelevant action is this introductory paragraph for a chapter heading that is self-explanatory. Straight to business:

Are You Intentionally Procrastinating?

There are certain cases where you knowingly delay a project. A lot of people usually say they are waiting for the 'right time.' Others say they want to get 'in the mood.'

Whatever your excuse, these are instances where you delay your projects on purpose. In other situations, it may be your willingness to complete tasks for other people rather than face your tasks. Although you may be helpful to these people, you are doing it at a cost.

In cases where you avoid your tasks, it is common for individuals to panic when the deadline starts getting close. Your state of panic is because you haven't done anything regarding the task. As a result, the job becomes an immediate emergency you must deal with. If you can identify these situations and accept that you are procrastinating, it becomes easy to overcome procrastination. Without proper identification of the reason for your procrastination, you cannot devise a suitable course of action to take in solving the problem.

The step to overcoming these time-wasting traits is to understand that you cannot wait for conditions that suit you before working on a project. You need to act immediately. Immediate action will also serve as motivation and prompt you to achieve more.

Avoid Multi-tasking

A lot of people may consider multi-tasking as a useful skill. When multi-tasking, an individual usually attempts to complete different tasks at the same time. It means they will have to continue shifting focus between various tasks until the tasks are complete. In truth, multi-tasking is usually effective when handling small tasks. For a more complex task, it is challenging to multi-task. In the end, it will take more time to complete the tasks.

If you attempt to divide your attention among various tasks, not only will you waste a reasonable amount of time, but you will also reduce your overall productivity. It is due to the unnecessary change in context that you will need to adapt to each time you move to a different task. Just because you appear to be very busy doesn't imply that you are making any reasonable progress in your task. Keep things simple. Focus on one task at a time. It will improve the quality of your output and productivity.

The Simple Yet Effective Methods to Cure Procrastination

Take Immediate Action

If there is a task that you need to attend to, why not act as soon as you receive the task? Putting the task aside for a later date easily leads to procrastination.

Addressing small tasks and minor issues as they crop up will prevent you from dealing with a large complex task in the future. It also becomes difficult to achieve your immediate goals if you still have tasks from the past that require your attention. A lot of individuals often use these tasks as an excuse not to handle their present tasks. You are more likely to complete a task once you start working on it. Therefore, you should avoid setting aside a task for another time. If you find a task that requires your attention, address it as soon as possible.

Remove Distractions That Are Around You

There are lots of things that can serve as distractions when working on a task. The most common form of distraction nowadays is your phone. Your computer can also be a huge distraction if you are not careful. Creating a unique workplace can also help to avoid distractions. When setting up this workplace, you need to eliminate all forms of distractions. It is also vital you identify anything that serves as a personal distraction to you.

A common distraction can be a window through which you can enjoy an outdoor view. It can also be a desk that is cluttered. If there is a window with an excellent view in your workplace, then turn your desk away from the window. If a cluttered desk can distract you, then clean up the desk and tidy up the area around to eliminate distractions. Since phones and computers can be a huge source of distraction, there are various steps you can take. You can choose to turn off Wi-Fi access on your phone and computer if the internet is a distraction. You can also disable notifications on both devices when working on a project.

If internet access is necessary for your work, then use software that can block access to social media sites or other web pages that can serve as distractions. To avoid completing a task, distractions are usually the best options. Once you can identify your personal distractions, it becomes easy to remove these distractions.

Develop Better Strategies for Handling Your Email

The most effective way to manage your email is to ensure that you organize and clean your inbox. Answering emails can be a significant time-waster if you don't adopt the right method to handle it effectively. Without a proper plan, you will become a slave to the notification bell that goes off as soon as you get a new message. Regardless of the task at hand, you will instinctively switch to the email before returning to the task at hand.

As a result, you lose focus, motivation, and momentum towards the task. Below are the specific steps you can take to handle emails effectively.

The Simple Yet Effective Methods to Cure Procrastination

Respond to All Your Emails Together

The same way you will handle tasks that are similar at the same time, you can also respond to your emails at the same time. You need to avoid responding to emails as they come in. By responding to emails at the same time, you can reduce your time spent on responding to each message.

Create Folders for Emails

It is possible to use a single account to manage various email addresses. It can be challenging to identify emails from each account without a label. To identify personal emails or business emails, you can use a filter and label on each address you manage on the account. To save time, you can attend to the business emails now and then go through your personal emails during your free time.

Short Emails Are Better

An email can be your work tool which you keep professional. To make it appear professional, you should make your email simple and straight to the point. Since you spend less time constructing your messages, you will have more time to spend going through other messages.

Allocate a Specific Time to Check Emails

Allocating a specific time to manage your email can be very beneficial. You can choose to check your email twice a day. The first time can be in the morning. During this period, you can respond to new messages that may have come in the previous day or earlier in the day. The second time can be after lunch. Having an automatic response can also help save time when responding to emails.

Prioritize

Prioritizing is an important step you take after breaking down a project into smaller tasks. It depends on how important each task on the list is to the overall project. As a result, you will be listing the items in descending order of importance. Using a color-coding system or a letter system can serve as a visual cue when prioritizing your tasks. Below are steps you can take when prioritizing:

- Create a list of all your activities the previous night.

- Identify the most important tasks on the list.

- What tasks are my personal tasks and what tasks are requests from others?

- What is the most difficult task on the list?

- What is the deadline for each task?

- How much effort do I require for each task?

As soon as you take these steps, it becomes easier to arrange your tasks by priority. There are a few things you should also do when prioritizing. You need to be flexible and avoid putting off personal goals.

The Simple Yet Effective Methods to Cure Procrastination

Using the Eisenhower Matrix to Prioritize

When prioritizing your tasks for the day, the Eisenhower Matrix can be very beneficial. It is also helpful in making quick decisions. It is a decision-making strategy introduced by Dwight Eisenhower. It is a principle that is suitable for addressing your tasks in order of importance and urgency.

There is a need for this principle since unexpected changes are bound to happen during your day. These changes may affect your plans for the day. The strategy is a simple way to deal with these random disruptions and minor emergencies. There are four quadrants in the Eisenhower Matrix, and each quadrant needs a unique strategy and approach to address it. The arrangement of tasks into each quadrant is based on the urgency of the task. Tasks that you should not include in your lists and those that you should delegate to others will also become easy to identify.

Quadrant 1 (Q1): Urgent and Important Tasks

The tasks that fall within the Q1 are those that you should address first. These are the tasks that have a significant impact on your career or life. They need to be completed immediately. Completing a project that is due by the end of the workday is a Q1 task. It may also be a reply to a time-sensitive message from a client.

Quadrant 2 (Q2): Important Tasks but Not Urgent

The tasks that fall within the Q2 are the tasks that are important but do not require immediate action. These are tasks that have a significant impact on the long-term goals you intend to achieve.

A professional course that will get a certificate you need to enhance your career will fall in this category. Taking the course is important to your career, but there is no deadline to achieve this goal. Overlooking the tasks in the Q2 is easy.

Quadrant 3 (Q3): Urgent Tasks but Not Important

When you say yes to all requests you get, it is easy to pile up some tasks that are urgent but not important to you. These are tasks that have no significant benefit to you. Tasks in the Q3 are easy to delegate to other individuals. It is important you delegate these tasks carefully. Distractions are the main reason why you end up thinking that a task is urgent. Giving immediate responses, using your phone, or reading emails are some common distractions that can get you here.

Quadrant 4 (Q4): Unimportant Without Urgency

The main time-wasting tasks that you need to avoid at all cost make up the Q4 of the matrix. Since you are looking for options to create more time, eliminating Q4 tasks is your best option. You can then reinvest the time you get from eliminating these tasks into more beneficial quadrants. It is important you understand that certain Q4 activities are necessary for your life. It is often a way to balance your work life with your professional life. Some Q4 tasks include scrolling through the internet, watching TV, and spending time with your family. Spending time with your family is a task that you should perform to balance your professional life. Watching TV may look like a good form of relaxation, but there is no significant benefit.

Time Management with a To-Do List

Create a To-Do List for Each Day of the Week
Planning is one of the most efficient ways to increase performance and productivity. Nonetheless, there are very few people who plan their day. With a To-Do list, you can simply plan your day with a paper and pen. Using technology, you can also incorporate time management apps to plan your activities every day.

Make It A Habit
When you repeat an action continuously, it slowly becomes a habit. The same applies to the use of a To-Do list. Always follow the activities on the list. You should also include any new activity that comes up to the list. A good step is to make your list the previous night or at the close of the day. The activities on the list that you are unable to achieve should come first on the list for the new day.

Create Your List the Previous Night
Sitting up the night before to create your lists is a sure way to improve your productivity. It is a way of planning. Your competence is a measure of how effectively you can make plans.

It is easier to rise above procrastination if you can develop excellent plans. You will also prepare yourself mentally for your goals. As you sleep, you will subconsciously go over the list, think of the best ways to achieve each goal, and wake up with new ideas on how to go about it. You will be able to work faster and more effectively.

Put A Check on Completed Tasks

As you progress each day, you will be completing the items on your list. Tick off each item to give a visual representation of your progress. It serves as motivation as you look at your success for the day. Visible progress improves your self-esteem and drives you to achieve more. It is an easy way to overcome procrastination.

Types of To-Do Lists

Depending on the purpose, there are variations of a To-Do list. The first type you will consider is a master list. It is a list that contains all the activities, tasks, and ideas that you have for the future.

The second type of list is your monthly list. It is a list that contains the activities for a new month. It is the list that you develop when sorting the master list. The weekly list is the third list. Here, you create plans for the week ahead. There may be changes that you will make to this list as the list progresses. The final list is the daily list. It consists of activities that you will be performing on a specific day. Items from your weekly and monthly lists usually make up your daily lists.

The Simple Yet Effective Methods to Cure Procrastination

The Importance of Saying No

Performing tasks for other people is a leading cause of time wasting. It is usually a result of saying YES to every request you get. In the end, you may end up stretching yourself too thin. If you can say NO to certain requests, you can get your time back. Now you have time to focus on things that are more important. It is also a way to avoid making promises that you cannot keep.

If you are the type that cannot say NO, there are certain things that you have accepted that don't give room for things that are important. It is why your schedule is usually full. It also makes you feel overwhelmed when other things crop up. You can save a lot of time by merely saying NO. It also saves you money when you learn to say no to that gym subscription you don't use.

What Can You Say No To?

There are lots of things that you can say NO to. It becomes easier to identify these things if you prioritize them. When looking to manage your time effectively, priorities play a vital role.

What are the things that you love doing? What are those things that matter most? What will be the effect if you don't do this task? As you begin to answer these questions, things become a lot easier. The items that are left on the list after answering these questions are your priorities. The others are not necessary. All you need to understand is that you need to give up certain things to achieve others. If you notice that your music lessons are preventing you from performing tasks relating to your job, you need to ask yourself a simple question – do you love your job? If the answer is yes, then you should give up music lessons for now so you can focus on the job.

The same also applies to what you do during your free time. Are you spending more time playing games than with your girlfriend? Do you love your girlfriend? If you don't want to lose her, you should be ready to reduce your gaming time to have more time with her. Since there are a limited number of hours in a day, you need to make some weighty decisions to make the most of these hours. Identify how you are spending your day and make changes. You can say no to almost anything as long as you have your priorities. Your priorities are the things that are important. Once you can focus on these priorities, you can say no to the things that don't matter.

Best Ways to Say NO

Avoid Giving an Instant Answer
Giving an instant answer will often lead to poor decisions. An immediate answer is usually a common response to any request you get when you are busy or distracted. Another easy way to identify an instant answer is to take note of requests you accept and then you instantly regret making that decision.

The Simple Yet Effective Methods to Cure Procrastination

How does it waste your time? We often spend a lot of time wishing we didn't accept a request. It is also common to waste some of our time trying to reschedule or backtrack on decisions. These are common methods of time wasting. Understanding when you are about to give an instant answer is important. Make sure you STOP before taking such decisions.

There are a few steps you can take to avoid making decisions in haste. First, you need to think about the request. Do you have time for the request? Do you really want to accept it? Answering these questions may require a pause but the time it takes is far less than what you spend backtracking.

Delay Your Reply

Buying yourself a bit of time before deciding can be very helpful. A simple response like, "Let me get back to you" is an excellent way to create time to think. It is much better than the regret that comes with an instant reply. Now, you have the time to check your schedule. Do you have time for this request? What time will be more convenient?

There is usually no rush with the response in this case. The other party will understand that you need to check with another individual or go through your schedule. There is also no specific time by which you need to decide. It gives you the time to think through your decision.

Avoid Digital Distractions

Social media, emails, and smart phones are the common digital distractions that often make it difficult to say no. How?

Once you appear to be online, people will assume you have some free time. Since this assumption implies that it is convenient for you, there will be more room for unnecessary distractions. Turning off your internet access is an easy way to lock out digital distractions. It is an excellent way to say no to interruptions. This is because you also make it difficult for people to get in touch with you while working.

Would You Do It Tomorrow?

Another easy way to say no to a request is to determine if it is a task you will want to do another day. Is it something you are passionate about? What does this imply?

Any task that you will be happy to work on tomorrow is a task that you are eager to work on. Then it is okay to say yes to such requests. If you feel you won't want to do this task tomorrow, then your best option will be to say no. Since there is no enthusiasm to do the task another day, it will become difficult to motivate yourself to perform the task. It is the reason you have the same task on your schedule for four weeks straight.

Move it to a More Convenient Time

There are certain situations where you may have an interest in the task before you, but you don't have enough time now. Then the proper line of action is to shift to a convenient time. To avoid commitment, don't accept the request but give the person a specific date to check with you again. In this case, you can avoid overloading your schedule while the other person will have this task on their To-Do list.

Don't Get in a Match with Time-Wasters

There are lots of people who know how to waste a lot of time on tasks. It can be on a complex task or a straightforward task. Time has no value to such individuals. These are the type of people that get a NO as an answer. If you avoid working with such individuals, you have the opportunity of saving your time and avoid stress.

So how do you identify a time waster? A common habit of most time wasters is to set up a meeting or call and then wait until the last minute to cancel the plans. The time you spend preparing for the meeting, adjusting your schedule to create room, or in some cases, the time taken to get to the meeting venue is already time wasted. Nonetheless, they still want you to make new plans.

Any person who sends unnecessarily long emails or anyone that agrees to a document being set it at a time and then fails is also a time waster. You should learn to say NO to such people. It gives you the opportunity to use your time for other valuable ventures.

Why You Are Always Exhausted

Freelancers and entrepreneurs are typical examples of people who experience burnout when they always say YES. It is often due to accepting any project from all clients. They usually have a fear that there will be no new work available.

In truth, if you don't say no to projects now and then, it can lead to exhaustion. You will also have to do a lot of work that you don't enjoy. It can be quite tricky to turn down projects as a freelancer. The same applies when turning down clients as an entrepreneur. You can start by saying NO to certain projects that you don't enjoy doing. As a result, there will be more time to fit in tasks and projects that you are passionate about.

Polite Ways to Say NO

One of the primary reasons why it is difficult for people to say no is the thought of offending others. If this is your main concern, then you can learn some polite ways to turn down people.

If you want to shift the task to the next week, you can reply with, "I simply haven't got time this week." It is also useful if you would like it after a month. You can also say:

- "It is a no I'm afraid. But thanks for asking me."

- "I simply haven't got the time right now."

- "I'd love to, but I've got other family commitments right now."

Chapter 4:
Get Organized and Productive Even with a Hectic Schedule

It can be tough to remain organized and productive when your schedule isn't giving you room to breathe. In such situations, you need to learn how to utilize the little time you have effectively. The two areas I will be discussing in this chapter are the time-boxing method and the use of digital tools. In the digital tools section, you will learn about some of the most important areas that require organization and how you can use technology for the best results.

Time-Boxing

What is Time-boxing?

It is a productivity technique that is useful in managing your time more effectively. The technique involves apportioning a specific time to an activity. You then complete the activity within the allotted timeframe. It is a technique that is simple on paper but can be very difficult to implement. Here we will be taking an in-depth look at the time-boxing technique. Below are some basic things you need to understand to apply the method effectively:

Types of Time-boxes

The time-boxing technique consists of soft time-boxes and hard time-boxes. Time-boxes are separated into these categories depending on the process required to handle it:

- The end of a soft time-box usually gives room for people to conclude and complete their current activities, tasks, or discussions.

- The end of a hard time-box requires people to stop immediately, go on a break, and then begin the event that comes next.

During a soft time-box, hearing the timer alarm implies that it is time to bring the task to a conclusive end. As it should, it notifies everyone that the time allotted to this task has been exhausted. Regardless, there is still room to keep working on the task or keep the discussion going. The soft box method is applicable in situations where the idea of time-boxing is just being introduced. It provides room for the necessary adjustments to take place.

The hard time-box is a much more iron-handed approach. It is also applicable in a situation where the idea is just being introduced, but it does not give room for an extension. In most cases, people will usually find out that they are unable to produce any meaningful result before the allotted time elapses. After experiencing a similar event a few times, it becomes easier to adjust work patterns. It also becomes a lot easier to work with the time allotted to a task. You must understand the type of time-box you will be applying and the reason.

Making Your Plan

Planning is an essential aspect of time-boxing. The plan should be laid out at an earlier time. It will make the technique more effective. How much time do you need for an activity? Certain activities and discussions can go on for a very long time if there is no limit to the time allotted. Failure to clearly state the duration of an activity will often lead to misplaced priorities. It is often the reason why some people fail to achieve the essential goals of the day. They spend too much time dwelling on the least important topics. By setting the time for a topic or activity in advance, you can avoid these issues. Using the time/value ratio can also be helpful in these situations. Sometimes, an impromptu meeting may come up in your workplace. These are meetings that usually don't have an agenda. It is essential you take a short time to come up with a clear agenda, with duration for each activity or topic on the agenda. Communication is also vital. If you have a speaker, you need to let them know the time duration for their session.

Making Your Time Visible

The time for each activity should be apparent to every member of the team. It means you need to use a timer app on your smart phone or a simple kitchen timer. To ensure that everyone knows the amount of time left, a countdown timer is more beneficial.

Avoid timers that utilize simple numbers to indicate the time left. Instead, opt for timers that offer a visual representation of the time. Although there is usually a moderator to monitor the time for each activity, a visual indicator of the time makes it possible for everyone on the team to function as a moderator. You will notice some people motioning towards the timer to get other members to focus. Since it is visible to everyone, it becomes easy for anyone to silence any chit-chat during an activity authoritatively.

What is the Maximum Length of a Time-Box?

An important question that people often ask when using the technique is the maximum length for an activity. What is the maximum length for a time-box? A maximum of forty-five minutes is suitable for an activity on the time-box. There are reasons for this choice. One such reason is that forty-five minutes aligns with the biological rhythm of the body. It is a fact that psychology also supports. It is the same reason why schools limit each period to forty-five minutes. When developing your time-box, you should not exceed the maximum of forty-five minutes. You should also include short breaks that can vary from five – fifteen minutes. If you have a topic that will require more than forty-five minutes, then using multiple time-boxes will be necessary.

Taking Breaks

To also support the maximum length of each activity, there should be a short break after this time duration. You can set a five-minute break after forty-five minutes or a fifteen-minute break after ninety minutes.

Another easy way to make plans is to set a fifteen minute-break after a forty-five-minute activity. Since the action and the break sum up to sixty minutes, it becomes easy to use a full hour for your activity planning. Avoid remaining on your seat during your break. It is an excellent time to get around, enjoy the sights, and get some fresh air. Do not indulge in activities like going through social media sites or checking your email. These will often make you remain on your chair.

It is also vital you make a clear announcement of the time the break will end. Stating that there is a five-minute break is not as specific as saying that the break will last till 2:50 pm. Most individuals don't look at their watch at the start of a break. Instead, they are more likely to check how much time they have left. Therefore, knowing the time, the break will end is more effective.

What is the Right Action When the Time is Exhausted?

Standing your ground when the time is up is important for the effectiveness of the time-boxing technique. Frustrations and panic are common reactions you can expect if a person is unable to complete a task within the allotted time. It may be tough to deal with early on, but you will learn to appreciate it over time.

When working with others, providing a warning is important. Letting others know two or three minutes before the time up offers ample time to conclude their work. A visual timer can also be of help, either a kitchen timer or a smart phone app. As soon as the time for an activity or task is up, you need to decide on the right step to take. The options available are to either create a new time-box for the current activity or go on to the next action. It all depends on you.

Do remember, it is necessary you avoid focusing on what may appear to be important. According to your time-boxing schedule, you have already made definite plans based on the importance of each activity. Stick to these plans. It may also be worth taking a few minutes to carefully consider if it is worth creating a new time-box for the activity. Your decision should be purely based on the strategic goals you intend to achieve.

Advantages of Time-boxing

There are lots of benefits to the use of this productivity technique. They include the following:

- It promotes the inclusion of regular breaks.

- The technique encourages people to come up with results.

- It helps in maintaining a focus on priorities.

- The development of results makes it possible to measure progress.

- It becomes possible to predict when the next activity will begin since you know when the current activity will end.

- Anyone has the power to end un-necessary discussions during work regardless of position.

- It is an excellent technique to improve productivity.

Downsides to The Use of Time-Boxing

Although time-boxing is important and beneficial to a lot of people, there are others who may not find it as appealing. It may often be due to certain jobs that require the best quality. These are tasks that you need to perform regardless of the amount of time it takes to complete. Using time-boxing in such situations can lower the quality of the output. Another clear case is the need to stop an activity and switch to the next as soon as the time is up. It can be challenging to do this if you are in the zone and fully immersed in the task. No-one will be willing to give up that momentum which usually makes it easy to come up with great ideas.

Following a strict schedule may often be very difficult for some individuals. It is usually due to interruptions in the form of a colleague walking up to your desk, phone calls, or other distractions.

Setting the right length of time for an activity can also be very difficult. An activity with excess time will often make it very easy to procrastinate. On the other hand, if the time is too short it reduces your chances of accomplishing any meaningful result. It is important you assess your speed on various types of tasks before creating a time-boxing schedule. You can then organize your activities accordingly. As powerful a tool as time-boxing is, it is only effective when used under the right set of conditions.

Using Digital Tools to Get Organized

Technology currently has a massive impact on how we perform different activities. The way you utilize technology can have a huge impact on your productivity. Learning about digital tools at your disposal can be very helpful. In this section, I will be discussing some very important productivity apps that you can easily use to organize your day and improve your productivity. To make things simpler, I have taken an extra step by creating different categories with similar apps.

Focus Apps

Focusing on your important tasks during the day can be very difficult with internet connectivity. That is why you need focus apps. These apps usually help in blocking some of the time-wasting sites you visit regularly. Apps in this category are suitable for people who prefer to be on social media sites like Instagram or Facebook instead of doing actual work. One of the excellent apps that you can use is:

StayFocusd

If you want to improve your discipline and focus, then you can try out the StayFocusd app. It functions as an extension on Google Chrome that limits the duration of your access to a site. There is a time allotted to a site for a day. You will be unable to access that specific site for the remainder of the day once you use up the allotted time. The blocking feature extends to specific pages, sites, in-page content like games, and subdomains. It promotes positive focus habits while blocking sites that waste your time during the day. Since there is a limit to how long you can use a website, it is suitable for individuals who like to keep some sites open in a browser tab. Other apps include:

- Freedom
- Focus
- Forest

Scheduling and Time Management Apps

The personality of individuals is often very different. Some people enjoy making plans and organizing their lives. For others, a little assistance will do a lot of good. In both cases, having an app that can help with scheduling and time management will be beneficial. They are suitable for making both short-term and long-term plans. Here is an app that falls within this category:

Todoist

This app allows users to take down notes like creating a text message quickly. The app then recognizes this message and creates a task by interpreting the text you input. Using a hashtag on the app makes it possible to group tasks into categories.

In a case where you have a text input that reads, "Visit the store for new games at seven p.m. tomorrow #gaming," the Todoist app will create a 7 p.m. reminder for the next day under the gaming category. There are also other additional features on the app including an option to integrate with more than sixty different apps. These include Slack, Dropbox, Amazon Alexa, and more. You can also choose to assign various tasks to people in a group using the app. Other similar apps in this category include:

- Taskful
- Blink
- Google Calendar
- Things

Personal Apps

When your own life gets stressful, messy, and disorganized, turning to a personal productivity app is your best option. These apps provide reminders of the essential things you need to do. They remind you of your errands, upcoming birthdays, and what you have on your grocery list. If you have a goal you want to achieve, you can also set it up on any of these apps. Some are available in the form of meditation apps that ensure that your stress levels remain in check. An app you can try out in this category is the popular Strides app.

Strides

Strides is an excellent option for achieving some essential life goals. It may be a good habit you are trying to develop or a bad habit you want to eliminate. It also allows users to set up routines that they would like to follow. To ensure that you are held accountable for your actions, the app features a SMART tracker. If you love visual representations, then you would enjoy the charts, red and green pace line system, as well as the reminders that the app offers.

If you want reminders of your daily routine in detail, Strides is a great option. Another great feature is that the app is free. Others that offer similar functions include:

- Google Keep
- Mindfulness
- Kiwake

Workplace Apps

Your workplace is supposed to be the place where you get a lot of work done. It is one of the easiest places to get distracted. Due to these distractions, you may be piling up a lot of work. The chances that you will lose focus and have low productivity usually increase when you have access to a computer throughout your work period.

Apps that promote productivity in the workplace help with team management, files and documents organization, communication with team members, and tracking your tasks. The apps in this category vary in terms of function, but I will be discussing the communication app – Slack.

Slack

Slack is an effective communication app that is suitable for team communications. Connecting with team members on Slack is easy. The app helps users build and connect with over 1,000 team members. You can build a channel for communication on the app. There is also a feature to give the channel a name based on the topic of discussion or team.

The channel you set up on the app may only include a select number of individuals or can be a company-wide channel. In addition to the channel messages, you can also send a direct message to any member on the channel. It is much faster than using email. The app also supports videos, photos, documents, and GIFs sharing. It is possible to integrate this app with Twitter, Dropbox, Google Drive, and lots of other apps you may use in the workplace. Other apps you can use include:

The Simple Yet Effective Methods to Cure Procrastination

- Trello
- LastPass
- Quip

Writing Apps

Writing apps are useful for taking quick notes to ensure you can recollect important information later. In addition to notes, you can also use these apps in creating To-Do lists. There is an increase in the efficiency of the note-taking, and information recording features these apps offer. You will often find exporting, editing, annotation, sharing, and organizing options on these apps. Evernote is a popular writing app available.

Evernote

The Evernote app is a hybrid of a planner and a notepad. It is an excellent option for creating a To-Do list and make short notes. The functions available on the app include document sharing, sketching, writing, and dictating notes. You can choose to create a checklist or plan an agenda. There are premium features that you can access by paying a monthly subscription. Nonetheless, it still offers excellent functionalities on the free version. The writing apps have a lot of features that are common, but there are also some with unique features. I would advise you also check these alternatives:

- Hemingway Editor

- Notability

- Bear

Meeting Apps

The meeting apps are those that help when you are trying to schedule a meet. It may be a workplace meeting, event planning, or social media event planning. It helps to eliminate back and forth during the scheduling process to makes things much more manageable.

Doodle

A major problem with scheduling a meeting is finding the time when everyone will be free. It often results in multiple emails going back and forth to fix a suitable date. In addition to being time-consuming, this process can be very inefficient. By making use of the Doodle app, you have the option of selecting some dates that will be preferable for the meeting. The invitees can then choose from the list of suggestions you send to them. By functioning through Whatsapp, iMessage, email, Facebook, and other options, the invitees don't need the Doodle app to select. To ensure that everyone is on the same page regarding the date, the app supports integration with a calendar.

Email Apps

One area where a lot of people have difficulties is in effectively managing their email. There are lots of new emails that come in every day. It may be a personal email, work-related email, special offer emails, or spam. To minimize the time and effort it takes to read through your emails and properly organize them; you can use any of the numerous email productivity apps available. Below are some of the apps available:

Trove

Trove is an email productivity app that provides functionalities that make it easy to organize your emails. It allows you to indicate what email requires your immediate attention and those that can wait till another time for a response. Users can categorize emails as Connect, Radar, or Nudge using flags. The flags serve as reminders indicating how you should deal with an email. Trove is an excellent option for individuals who get a lot of emails daily. There are other email apps you can try out if necessary, including:

- Newton
- Astro

Voice-to-Text Apps

As the name implies, these are apps that assist in transcribing audio. It is a great feature that helps when you must go to a lecture. It is quite common to find a few lecturers that don't give you enough time to keep up when handwriting.

Otter

As a student or a journalist, you can't underestimate the benefits of this note-taking app. It functions through the combination of transcription, audio, and speaker identification. It is a good app for days when you would rather listen than take notes. Using voice identification, it can identify the various speakers if there is more than one. The transcription option is also designed for the long lecture and conversations in the long-form. There is a free account that offers 600 minutes of free transcription while the premium account offers a recording time of 6,000 minutes.

Chapter 5:
The Secret to Become Motivated

Motivation is the set of needs and desires that drive an individual to take a particular action. Motivation can be intrinsic or extrinsic. The importance of motivation is to strengthen your behavior towards achieving a specific goal. There are different ways to get motivated. Read on to find out how.

Discover Your Passion
One of the easiest ways to get motivated is to do something you are passionate about. In most cases, you do things you are passionate about not for what you can gain, but for the meaning it brings to your life. It is easy to lose motivation when you are performing a task for the money involved. Setting your sights on only what you can gain will make you lose sight of why it is crucial.

Regardless of what you are doing, there will be days when you are feeling low. You may be low on energy, ideas, or inspiration. It doesn't matter if it is something you are passionate about or not. Doing things, you are passionate about will make it easy to persevere through these low periods.

Willpower

The ability of an individual to complete a task is what I refer to as willpower. It is the ease with which you can perform a task. Like the muscles of the body, willpower is a thing that you can relax and flex when necessary. You lose the ability to make the most of it when you fail to use it often. You can also make it more powerful through practice and training. It is also possible to weaken your willpower when you depend on it excessively during your daily work periods. There are two significant steps you can take to improve the way you utilize your willpower. They include the following:

Increasing Your Willpower

Similar to how you strengthen muscles, you can also strengthen your willpower. To push your willpower to its limits, you need to discipline your mind. It is also important you take proper care of your health. As a result, your willpower becomes stronger and higher.

Minimize Your Dependence on Willpower

Just because you have enough doesn't mean you should waste it. There are other easier ways to make it more effective. It is also like how we avoid overworking the muscles. Although you may be strong enough to carry all your purchases at a grocery store, a trolley can ease this task. With willpower, certain tricks help to minimize the amount of willpower you require to perform specific tasks.

How to Increase Your Willpower

The Simple Yet Effective Methods to Cure Procrastination

The problem with a lot of individuals is that they don't understand that they have weak willpower. If you don't believe it, then try studying without responding to a social media message. Changing your career, starting an exercise routine, visiting the gym more often, or simply learning a new skill are some arduous tasks that often expose a weak-willed individual. It is the reason you need to develop strong willpower.

When this is all said, how do you develop strong willpower? It is important to understand that willpower is not something physical. As a result, you will be applying some methods that may seem somewhat unconventional. Since it depends mainly on your physical and mental health, using the tricks below will help in developing strong willpower.

Performing Exercise
Inactivity of the body will also lead to the inactivity of the brain. It means that the brain will shut down as the musculature shuts down during prolonged periods of inactivity. A musculature that remains active will provide the necessary support that the brain needs to function efficiently. The support is in the form of efficient blood flow to the brain. In offices, a new strategy to ensure that the body remains active is using standing desks.

If you don't have access to a standing desk, taking shorts breaks during which you move around can be very beneficial. To exercise the body doesn't necessarily mean you need to perform strenuous activities. All you need is for the body to be active. Tweaking your daily schedule to include an activity is an easy way to meet this requirement. There are easy activities you can include in your schedule. It may be standing in certain situations where you usually sit or using the stairs instead of an elevator. Getting a minimum of 10,000 steps in a day can also be very helpful.

Any activity you enjoy that will engage the entire body is suitable for this process. It is the easiest way to replenish and increase your willpower for the day. A walk is one of the easiest activities you can perform. It is also the best option when you are trying to get work done, but you feel completely exhausted. A simple five-minute walk around the office will have you feeling a lot better.

Maintaining Good Health and Diet

There are various downsides to having an unhealthy body. One of them is an unhealthy brain. The brain is not only the most important organ of the body; it is also the most complex. It requires a lot of attention. When the brain is in a poor health condition, the impulse control of the body also becomes weaker.

The feeling of sluggishness you may be experiencing may be as a result of blood sugar fluctuations. The fluctuations are often an effect of being overweight or having a high Body Mass Index. These are both noticeable signs of an unhealthy body.

Sluggishness usually makes it more difficult to start a task, as well as see it through to the end. In addition to weight, a lack of micronutrients such as Vitamin D also affects the willpower of an individual. In this case, cognitive performance is usually the target. Keeping the body in a healthy condition will provide the necessary increase in willpower that you desire.

Getting Adequate Sleep

Sleep is crucial when topping off your willpower or increasing the limit. Its effects become noticeable when you apply it in combination with exercise and a good diet. Getting less than the recommended seven-eight hours of sleep per night is referred to as sleep deprivation. It is a situation which results in a lack of willpower. In more understandable terms, your mental functions will operate at a level like that of a drunken individual. There will be a negative impact on your willpower by just a single day of sleep deprivation. If you can get the full seven-eight hours rest per night, you can replenish your willpower to its peak levels. Besides, you also improve your productivity during the day.

Learn the Techniques of Meditation

Another popular method of increasing your willpower is through meditation. The importance of willpower is to help improve your focus and avoid distractions. When you meditate, it is a way of training the mind to focus. You train it to be able to maintain concentration on a small part of your life. It may be focusing on a mantra, your breath, or a point in the body.

Learning to focus on intangible things like your breath makes it easier to use your willpower to focus on the task directly in front of you. Another benefit of meditation is the complete control of your emotions. Temptation, anger, and frustration are some of your emotions that hinder your focus. When you meditate, you can allow these emotions to pass freely and then redirect your focus to what is important.

Stay Hydrated

Water intake is very important to us as human beings. A lot of us only understand its importance in keeping the body function. Water is also very valuable in maintaining your willpower. The cognitive functions of an individual can be negatively affected when dehydration sets in. Daily, you should consume at least eight glasses of water. It is equivalent to two liters.

Aim directly for your target, and you may come up short. The same applies in this case. It is better to aim for one gallon per day so you will be able to get past the minimum. In addition to increasing and maintaining your willpower, staying hydrated also helps in maintaining your weight by reducing hunger and improves the appearance of the skin.

Practice More

Your willpower is something that can be improved through practice. Repeatedly testing your limits will provide the necessary improvements you desire. There are lots of minor activities that can help in testing your willpower. Once you can complete these activities, you will observe improvements in your willpower.

Activities you can perform include resisting the urge to use your smart phone during a meal, going to bed early instead of watching another episode of your favorite series, drinking water in the morning instead of coffee, etc. Simple activities that are contrary to your bad habits are the best when it comes to strengthening your willpower.

Reducing Your Willpower Requirement

Like all important resources in the world, you must be careful about how you make use of your willpower. Just because your storage is full doesn't mean it won't go empty. To avoid using up your willpower quickly, you need to learn how to manage it throughout the day. There are different ways to avoid using up too much willpower on a single task. The strategies below will help in using only the necessary amount of willpower so you have enough for other tasks that may come up.

Split Larger Processes into Smaller Inputs

Intimidation is often an easy way to lose willpower. It is easy to become intimidated when you look at a project or task you are about to undertake, and the scope is more comprehensive than you imagine. It is like how it seems impossible to upload one blog post every week.

Simply split the larger task into smaller parts. For example, you can decide to write a 300-word paragraph of your blog post every day.

At the end of 5 days, you will have a blog post with 1,500 words. As a result, the overall task becomes easier to tackle. You will require a ton of willpower to start a project or task that appears to be intimidating. When you break it down into smaller parts, you drastically reduce the amount of willpower you require.

Develop a Habit

What makes habits so important? They are activities you engage in sub-consciously. A sub-conscious activity doesn't require you to decide. Your body automatically knows that it is the right action to take at that time. A good habit you can develop is to make your bed as soon as you wake up in the morning, head to the bathroom, and wash your mouth. Once these activities become a habit, you require less effort to complete them every day. It also provides the opportunity to think about other things. Developing good habits is an easy way to conserve your willpower for the rest of the day.

Consider your commute to work every day. You may decide to develop the habit of reading the morning news before getting to work. If you can repeat this activity for a week, it becomes a habit, and you don't require any willpower to read the news on your way to work.

When creating a habit that will conserve your willpower, always consider your most demanding tasks. You can decide to develop a habit of completing the most challenging task of the day as soon as you get to the office. You may also add a condition that you can only go through your mail once the job is complete.

Committing to a habit can be very difficult during the initial stages. To make it easier to commit, you should learn to use commitment apps like Stickk and Beeminder. It is also important to remember that you can also develop bad habits. These may have an adverse effect of reducing your willpower.

How Is Your Environment?

An easy way to maximize your willpower is to create an environment that minimizes its need. You will have more willpower if you don't need to use it frequently. What does it mean to create an environment to support your willpower? It is quite simple. A pull-up bar at the entrance of your office will reduce the willpower you require to perform a pull-up. In the same regard, you will use up a lot of willpower trying to resist using your phone if it is on your office desk and you keep hearing the notifications beep. If technology is a significant hindrance to your work, you can use certain apps to create a suitable environment. Apps like Freedom and RescueTime can help block certain sites to prevent access while working. Using Time-boxing techniques can also assist when you need to focus on a task.

Removing anything that may act as a distraction like your phone, your candy bars, or magazines can be very helpful. It is easier to forget about some things when they are not visible.

Using the If-Then Technique

When using this technique, you use an activity to serve as a trigger for another activity. It is also another excellent way to reduce the amount of willpower you require for a task. In this case, you create certain conditions like, "If I complete my first task at the office, then I can go through my emails." It is a simple condition that reduces the amount of willpower you require to focus on the present task. You understand that the only way you can check your emails is by completing the first task of the day.

As humans, we like to stay true to our words. Sometimes, having two contradictory ideas can be quite difficult. It is the reason why you are inclined to follow the conditions you have set. It is in a bid to prevent cognitive dissonance according to psychology. This technique implies that you can quickly begin a difficult task by creating a trigger using a much simpler task.

Understanding the Body Rhythms

At what time do you do your best work? At what time does your body need to take a break? How long can you go without using your phone? What is your circadian rhythm?

Understanding these types of questions is an easy way to become self-aware. According to the circadian rhythm, a lot of people lose some of their energy at about 2 p.m. while they experience the most fatigue at around 2 a.m. By learning what your circadian rhythm is, you can avoid excessive use of willpower during these periods. You can also reduce the amount of willpower you need for a task by learning about your ultradian rhythm. The ultradian rhythm regulates peak alertness and low alertness over a 90-minute cycle. Picking the peak periods to complete a task will reduce the willpower requirements for the task.

Don't Get Dragged into Hearing Bad News

The state of your mind can directly affect your willpower. An unhealthy state of mind is often a result of an unhealthy body. Other things that may result in an unhealthy state of mind include stress, sadness, and other negative emotions. Stress and sadness can often result from the type of information you consume. Information is available from various sources. It may be from a colleague, newspapers, social media sites, blogs, and other platforms.

Information that contains details on a downward trend in the markets, homicides in your neighborhood, or a bombing in a well-known city will often lower your willpower. Another easy way to lower your willpower is to go through the Instagram profile of a friend that is more successful. You may find pictures of exotic cars or a vacation to a Caribbean island. In truth, a lot of us are guilty of this action.

Learning to avoid these sources of bad news can be very helpful. The bad news you are getting in these situations have no direct impact on the decisions you will be making during the day. The information you need to learn about as a Forex trader includes the market movement. Any information relating to the life of a celebrity is irrelevant.

Develop a Personal Mantra

Having a personal mantra can be very helpful to motivate yourself to complete a task. It is an inspiration to be the best you can be and an affirmation of your great qualities. In general, a personal mantra is a statement or phrase that positively affirms the direction you want in life. When finding a way to achieve a goal, a personal mantra can encourage and motivate you to focus.

A personal mantra is only beneficial when it is visible and audible. Your mantra can also serve as a guide for your thoughts. If you are trying to lose weight but are currently thinking of taking junk food, an excellent personal mantra can be, "I am on the path to fitness, and my healthy body is my pride." To create a personal mantra, you need to do some thinking. It should be based on philosophy. Attaching a quote that you create or a quote from someone else is also important. The quote should be short and serve as a representation of the philosophy you have chosen.

Write down the mantra on a piece of paper that you will be able to see every day. You should also set aside a time each day when you read the mantra and make it a part of you. You should be reminded of your feelings every time you read your mantra. It should also reaffirm your beliefs in a case where you are slowly beginning to self-doubt.

The Simple Yet Effective Methods to Cure Procrastination

Have a Hunger That Is Insatiable

What is the difference between a person that violently goes after a goal and another that gives up on a goal as soon as things become difficult? This is a question that applies to goal-getting as well as completing a task. It is something that you notice when you take the time to study human behavior in different situations.

A lot of successful individuals have an insatiable hunger. It is this hunger that keeps driving them when things get difficult. It is what serves as their motivation in tough times. Regardless of the setbacks and failures that some people face, they usually remain focused on achieving their goals. The ability to learn from failures, rise, and keep going is what makes them unique.

There are various things that you will get from an insatiable hunger. It will feed you images and thoughts of your success. It will also help in the elimination of self-doubt. Developing an insatiable hunger is like creating an inner conviction you follow. You can build this conviction based on people who have achieved a similar feat.

You keep asking yourself questions like; "What are the changes I want that I can get from achieving this goal?", "What kind of person will I become after attaining it?", "Why is it so important to achieve it?" Every time you answer this question, it motivates you to push forward towards the goal.

Werner K. Clark

To build an insatiable hunger that will serve as motivation, you must be willing to adapt. Learn the best way to go from the challenges of life. Your motivation will usually come from your devotion to your goal. To remain motivated by your goal, it must provide meaning and purpose to your life. When a goal can provide these qualities, you will always have the motivation to achieve it.

Chapter 6:
Guaranteed Tricks to Make Habits Stick

Making a habit stick is a critical task. There are easy ways to make a habit but how do you make it stick? The steps below will lead you to that goal. They are all smaller parts of the more extensive process that you need to follow.

Start Small

When you are trying to make a habit that will stick, it is best to start very small. The mistake a lot of people make is trying to produce a huge change rapidly. Trying to achieve something large too fast will make it easy to give up on your goal.

Using the Seinfeld Calendar Strategy

It is difficult to stop doing an activity when you notice you have invested a lot of resources into the project. It can be a new blog post, a video mash-up, or a computer code. The same applies to your habits. If you can visualize the effort you have put into developing this habit, it becomes more difficult to break.

A simple strategy that applies to this situation is the 'don't break the chain' strategy that Jerry Seinfeld uses. In his description, he was trying to become a better comic by creating a joke each day. Once he achieved the goal for the day, he made a large 'X' on that day on the calendar. From this description, we can visualize two clear concepts. The first is a visual representation of your achievements. The second is a chain that is formed by crossing consecutive days with an 'X.'

You can use this strategy for any new habit you want to stick. As it becomes visible that you are on a roll from your calendar, you will be struggling to keep it that way. As a result, it becomes more difficult to break that habit. Every day you wake up without motivation to repeat any activity you set, the large crosses on the calendar serve as a reminder. It reminds you of the time and effort you put in to get so many crosses on the calendar. As a result, you will be motivated to repeat the activity. The longer your chain grows on the calendar, the easier it becomes to perform the activity. Repetition of the same activity over time will result in a habit that is difficult to break.

Use Implementation Intention

Implementation intention refers to the use of 'if-then' statements in developing your habits. It is an advantageous strategy since it doesn't depend on willpower to achieve results. The implementation intention will require you to create a link between the habit you want to develop and the activity you do regularly. By attaching a developing habit to an already established routine, it becomes easier to trigger your action.

Develop Keystone Habits with Goals Attached

It is easier to give up on a habit if there is no goal behind the habit. What is the long-term benefit of the habit? Is there a goal you will be able to achieve once you can form the habit? Setting goals in your mind is not the same as writing out your goals. By writing out your goals, you are creating a physical manifestation of the things you want to achieve. If they remain in the abstract world, it becomes easier to change them without any consequence.

When writing out your goals, be clear in the intent. What do you want to achieve? When do you want to achieve it? How do you want to achieve it? Why do you want to achieve it? Now you know the goals you have in mind. What are the habits that can help in achieving these goals? You should look for keystone habits that will help you achieve your goal at a much faster speed.

A keystone habit is merely a habit that produces a reaction that leads to the formation of other positive habits. Developing many keystone habits will produce other good habits in the long-run. It will also help in eliminating some of your current negative habits.

An example of a keystone habit is saving money. By saving money, you also develop the habit of spending on things that matter. It is because you know that your savings are only for emergencies and not for your daily spending.

You also learn to live within your means. Since you will be managing the little that is left after removing your savings, it becomes easy to live a life without borrowing. Although keystone habits usually have far more benefits, they do not require any additional effort to develop.

The first step is to list out the keystone habits that can help in achieving the goals you have set. The next step is to pay more attention to these habits during the early stages. In time, you will be able to reap more benefits from these habits.

Supportive People Should Be Around You

The way you behave is often a result of the people around you. If you have a friend that spends a lot of time studying, you will also find it easy to study. Distance is usually not a limitation to the support you get from friends. It is also common to choose goals that are like those of the people that are around you the most. So, if you want to be successful at a habit, you need people working on the same habits around.

For people who have friends with undesirable habits, it is crucial you find new friends with the habits you desire. The same applies to friends who are pessimistic. The negative comments from these individuals will have an adverse effect on your progress. Be selective of the five closest people around you. They usually have a significant impact on your behavior. Create a support group consisting of individuals that will serve as an inspiration and help you get back on your feet when you fall.

Pre-Commitment Is Necessary

By pre-committing to a habit, you are cutting off your escape routes. It means you have no option but to perform the habit or there will be consequences. A good example will be going jogging with a friend. If you agree to meet at 7:00 am, it becomes difficult to cancel your jog at the last minute. A lot of people wake up and change plans to their benefits once they start over-thinking. In truth, the lack of consequences for changing plans makes it very easy.

It is the same way you end up arriving late to a meeting after hitting the snooze button multiple times. "I'm feeling very tired. I still have enough time to rest for five more minutes. This will be the last time I hit the snooze button." In this case, if you have a friend that you agreed to meet at the bus stop at a specific time, it becomes easier to get up, so you don't delay.

In some cases, people pre-commit through a payment that they forfeit every time they fail to perform an activity. What better way to motivate yourself than to put some money on the one? Publicly announcing your daily targets is also a form of pre-commitment. Now you are accountable to your family and friends. To avoid making up excuses when people ask questions, you will want to perform these habits. It quickly becomes effortless to perform these tasks once you apply one or all these pre-commitment strategies.

Make Changes to the Environment

Your environment often determines how you behave. Designing your environment to promote the desired habit can be very helpful. A simple example is developing a habit of doing pull-ups. What do you think is the best method through which your environment can help you develop this habit? In this case, simply installing a pull-up bar at the entrance of your office will serve as your motivation.

It is a simple process that works in the same way as eating food simply because it is set in front of you. Understanding that your environment is the best tool to support your habit and using it to your advantage will help you effectively develop the habit. Taking deliberate steps to develop these habits will improve your chances of rapidly developing the desired habit.

Activation energy is also an important term you need to understand. It implies that there is a specific amount of energy that is necessary to perform a habit. A habit that requires high activation energy is usually more difficult to achieve. Reducing the activation energy is usually very important. For example, when learning to do pull-ups, you may find it easy to ignore the bar when stepping into your office space. The following steps can help:

- Reduce the activation energy by installing a pull-up bar at the entrance of your office space.

- Lock your office door before leaving.

- Place the key on the pull-up bar (to reduce the activation energy to reach for the pull-up bar).

It is an easy way to shift your attention towards the pull-up bar at the entrance of your office.

Negative Thoughts Should Be Eliminated

Negative self-talk is one way to derail your progress. It also causes the mind to develop a defeatist mindset. You start having more than a thousand thoughts that overshadow your goals, dreams, and hopes. Canceling all forms of negative self-talk is an essential step to take when developing habits that will stick. Questions that start with, "I don't think I can..." or "What if I can't..." are common forms of negative talk.

It is common to consider yourself to be unworthy of certain achievements. These include career, money, weight loss, and relationships. It may simply be thoughts that you do not deserve the things that you currently have. This is a flaw that is common to all humans. It is an imperfection that is inherent to us as individuals. Your primary objective is to be happy with the things you are doing and those you can achieve.

A simple way to get over your negative thoughts is to write them down. As soon as you write them down, you can re-phrase these thoughts into positive scripts. You should also give reasons why these negative thoughts don't apply to you. If a situation should arise where you find yourself getting overwhelmed with negative thoughts, take out your positive scripts. Repeat the sayings on the script to eliminate the negative thoughts.

What Is Your Inspiration?

Having other people to inspire you is a great way to make habits stick. What serves as the source of your motivation for this habit? Do you have any individual that encourages you? Is there anything that motivates you? Develop a vision around the answers to these questions. You should also create a board where you can place your vision. The board will serve as a reminder.

The board should be in a place where you can easily notice it every day. Attaching images to the board along with quotes can also serve as excellent reminders. Compiling visual aids that relate to your vision will also play a vital role in the impact of the visuals. The visuals may be images of places, things, or people.

Since you will see it daily, it will serve as your constant reminder of the reason behind a habit. It becomes possible to subconsciously think about what you intend to achieve and the steps you will take to achieve these goals. The only way you can keep working towards developing a habit is to have something always to remind you about that habit.

Develop One Habit at a Time

A habit is often key to personal development. Sticking to a habit is often vital for anyone that is looking to make progress in life. Selecting one habit to change at a time is usually a better option if you intend to make progress when developing a habit.

Consider a situation where you are looking to start going to the gym, making changes to your diet, and maintaining your weight. These are three new habits you intend to develop. Trying to do these three things at the same time can prove to be overwhelming. On the other hand, you can create a list of the habits you intend to develop. After making your list, you can then pick one habit to focus on developing. It becomes easier to plan and then work towards that habit. In the situation we are considering, your first step will be to make changes to your diet. Developing this habit will make it easy to feed your body correctly with healthy foods. Eating healthy will make it possible to lose weight. As a result, you will have the motivation to start going to the gym to maintain the weight you have worked hard to achieve.

Reward Yourself

It is common to find a lot of people who consider rewarding themselves anytime they make a meaningful achievement. It is a useful tip, but most of these individuals use it in a wrong manner. When developing a habit, proper use of rewards is a sure way to make such habits stick.

If you decide to give yourself a large reward for your progress, it can be harmful. It is also better you avoid rewards that come at the end of the week or month. Examples of large rewards include a vacation, a new gaming console, or new clothes. These are harmful to the development of habits that stick. Why? Using large rewards makes it easy for you to translate this reward into a prize. A prize is something you set out to win when performing an activity. A reward, on the other hand, is not the focus of developing the habit. An individual that is trying to develop a habit to gain the reward has a higher chance of quitting. Habits in most cases are difficult to create. What if an individual measure the reward in comparison to the stress that it takes to develop the habit? – It is easy to conclude that it is not worth the effort.

Taking steps to develop a habit for the reward also implies that you won't be willing to perform the next step if there is no reward. Regardless of the passion you have for an activity, it is easy to lose motivation when rewards are put into the equation. When selecting a good reward for your progress, there are certain things to consider. Below are some features of good rewards:

- They are small.

- They relate to the activity.

- You receive them immediately you complete the activity.

They Are Small
Having a larger reward always appeals to us as humans. A larger reward is often a great motivation to carry out a task or perform an activity. That is what makes it a problem when developing a habit that will stick. As a motivation for performing an activity, it means that without the reward you won't be inclined to repeat the activity. Your thoughts will align with phrases like, "I am doing it for the reward."

They Relate to the Activity
The reward for any action done should have a direct relationship to the action. In simpler terms, the reward should only be available if you can complete a particular action.

You Receive Them Immediately You Complete the Activity
One significant importance of a reward is to reinforce a behavior. For this reason, it is important you receive the reward immediately after the behavior. If you decide to wait till the end of the day to give the reward, it becomes difficult to identify the behavior you want to reinforce.

By receiving a reward immediately after an action, you will feel good about these actions. It promotes immediate recognition of an accomplishment. The functioning of the brain also makes an immediate reward important. The response of the brain to a reward is instantaneous. To make a habit that will stick, you want the brain to associate this reward to the activity you have completed at that instant.

Chapter 7:
The 5 Non-Obvious Things That Kill Your Productivity

Most of the things that kill our productivity are buried right under our noses. They have become an integral part of our daily lives, so it is difficult to notice them. In this chapter, I will be exposing some of these things that reduce your productivity without you noticing.

Your Bad Habits

One of the non-obvious things that kill productivity is habits. The many bad habits you have developed are steadily killing your productivity. They remain unnoticeable because these habits have become a vital part of your daily life. There are different ways through which your bad habits can reduce productivity. Here are some you may be experiencing.

Your Bad Habit of Not Making Lists

There are numerous benefits of a list in the workplace and the home. It helps you to remember the essential things that need to be done. It is also vital if you need to prioritize your tasks. Your reluctance to create lists of your daily tasks will often result in you forgetting some of the most critical tasks of the day. Have you ever gone to the grocery store and missed a few vital items?

Your Bad Habit of Being Overly Independent

Being independent is not a bad thing. It only becomes a problem when you are unable to meet up with urgent deadlines. In the workplace, working in a team is often very important. It provides the opportunity to delegate different aspects of a project to different people. It makes it easy to meet targets faster and meet deadlines. An easy way to avoid this bad habit is by starting to rely more on friends, family, employees, and co-workers.

Frugality as a Bad Habit

Frugality is one F the few habits you may have developed that may not seem like a problem. It can be a serious issue if you take it too far. If you decide to be frugal and avoid upgrading your work computer or programs, you end up with obsolete work tools. When your work tools become outdated, you start to lose a lot of time either from the slow boot-up of the computer or the slow response of the programs.

Not Getting Enough Sleep

Nowadays, the amount of sleep you get usually has a significant impact on your level of productivity. To create more time to work, a lot of people often sacrifice their long hours of sleep. As a result, they are killing their productivity without noticing. Just a single day of sleep deprivation can have damaging effects. These effects include poor judgment and an inability to retain information. If sleep deprivation becomes a consistent part of your life, there are other effects such as cardiovascular diseases, diabetes, and obesity.

Sometimes you may know about the importance of getting enough sleep but find it difficult to go to bed early. You must create a habit. Through the development of this habit, you will be able to go to bed as soon as the time is right. The necessary performance boost you have been searching for is usually hidden beneath a good night's rest.

Poor Health Diet

ANOTHER NON-OBVIOUS killer of productivity is your diet. Certain foods are killing your productivity that you don't know about. Below, I will be discussing these foods so you can get a better understanding of why you need to avoid them. Things you should avoid include:

- Eating in excess.
- Too much processed and frozen foods.
- Intake of fluid in an improper manner.
- Consuming too much caffeine in the morning.
- Failure to take snacks between meals.
- Excess junk food items.

Access to Technology

Technology is currently affecting our daily lives in lots of different ways. You have a computer, smart phones, internet, and many more. As helpful as technology is, it may sometimes be a subtle killer of your productivity. Here are different ways it results in lower productivity:

Your Computer

A computer can kill your productivity with its slow performance. It results in downtime while you wait for data transfers to be complete. It will also delay you and prevent work from being done when trying to open a program. The non-obvious ways it kills your productivity is noticeable in the shift in focus while waiting. Now you are concentrated on the discussion you are having with a colleague or the messages you need to reply on your smart phone. It is now necessary for you to think before you can know the next step to take.

Sometimes, the systems you use may be getting outdated or running older versions of important software. If there is no plan for a replacement or an upgrade, a sudden failure will result in downtime. The time it takes to fix this sudden breakdown is often more than the time spent when it is planned. It is important that software for business purposes should be updated. It is also necessary to plan for replacements of computers in the workplace. Using the expected life of the unit is an easy way to determine when replacements are due.

How You Use Your Smartphone

The Simple Yet Effective Methods to Cure Procrastination

Hands down, smart phones are easily one of the best inventions in the world. Nonetheless, if they are not handled properly, they can also be very destructive. In the workplace, smart phones offer the easiest form of distraction. Using your smart phone when you are supposed to be working is bound to have an adverse effect on your productivity.

It may be to check a personal email, visit a social media page, or reply to messages. Regardless of the reason, smart phones usually make it easy to lose focus. To solve this problem, you should keep your smart phone in a place that is difficult to see. If it is out of sight, it becomes out of mind. Your productivity at your work should be a priority. Using a smart phone will change this priority.

Distractions from Emails

If you get distracted easily, then you will have gone to your email to refresh it at one point. It is quite common with individuals who don't have a specific time for checking emails. It is one of the most subtle killers of productivity at work. Why? It has the appearance that you are performing a productive activity. It is a reasonable misinterpretation since you might be expecting a reply from a client. To deal with this problem, turning off your internet connection may not be the best solution since you may need it to work. Instead, create time on your schedule during which you check your emails. You should also close the email tab and disable notifications to avoid distractions.

Social Media

Connecting with people is a great way to create social relationships. That is the primary function of social media. It also helps to grow your network for business purposes. Although it has its benefits, social media is also a productivity killer at work. A notification pop-up on your screen will often take your attention away from your work. Falling for this trap and opening the social media site will also have its effects. It wastes time since you will end up scrolling down the timeline to find out what is new. Friends on social media sites also find it convenient to send messages when you appear online.

To avoid this non-obvious productivity killer at work, you can use site blocking apps to prevent access to social media sites during work sessions. You should also have a time that you will visit these sites.

Clutter

Clutter in your workplace and the home hurts your productivity. Your ability to work, mood, and resilience usually suffer from the effects of clutter. It is also possible to develop high-stress levels from the disorderliness that clutter creates. Mental and emotional distresses are common effects of clutter in the home environment. An individual may feel that he/she has no control over their lives due to the clutter around them. Distraction is one of the few effects clutter has on you. It also impedes the ability to process new information by the brain. As a result, you are unable to perform efficiently. It is difficult to fight all the distractions that are present due to a cluttered environment.

The Simple Yet Effective Methods to Cure Procrastination

It depletes your mental energy, reduces physical energy, and causes frustration. When you are frustrated, you end up being unproductive.

If you fail to find a solution to the clutter around you, you may end up lowering your self-esteem. It often causes both emotional and mental discomfort. In most cases, addressing the clutter around may require a ton of energy. It is effortless to avoid it as a result. The clutter may end up spiraling out of control if you are unable to find a solution early. Below are some of the areas where you need to focus on when addressing clutter:

Clutter Can Be in Digital Form

Digital clutter is usually present on your phone, tablet, or computer. A digital clutter may be notifications or files that require your immediate attention. Your productivity when using your computer or smart phone depends on how easy it is to use and its functionality. Having many files on these devices can make it difficult to locate important files when you need them. Having too many files to check through will often reduce the effectiveness of the brain. It leads to a poor job and a reduction in your productivity levels.

Your Home

The home is the place where you start your day. Having an uncluttered home can help with the enhancement of your mental and emotional health. Removing clutter from the home may seem overwhelming. In truth, it is much easier if you break the task into smaller parts.

You may decide to clear the clutter room by room. You may also choose to address it according to categories from your cutlery to laundry and so on. A much faster way to ensure that items causing clutter don't find their way back into the home is to throw out a few, sell some, and give away the rest. You should also look for options that allow you to recycle some of these items. Selling items, you don't need is always an easy way to make extra cash for more important things.

Your Workspace

Your workspace is where you perform your important tasks for the day. It may be your home office or your desk in an office building. Clutter in your workplace consists of all those unnecessary items taking up space on your desk. As a source of distraction, your brain will have to expend more energy to ignore these distractions. It makes you exhausted a lot faster with a direct impact on your productivity. To clear the clutter on your desk, you will need to create time. You may have to pick a few days during which you won't be going out for lunch. You will be spending this time organizing your desk and workspace.

Some items that you should clear out from your desk include old magazines, outdated files, and books that you enjoy reading often. Other items that are now irrelevant should also be cleared out. In addition to improving your productivity, a desk that is free from clutter will also have an attractive appearance and provide motivation.

The Simple Yet Effective Methods to Cure Procrastination

Your Mind

We have discussed digital and physical clutter but what about clutter in your mind? Clutter in the mind may often be due to unnecessary information that you are storing but have no use for. Learning ways to get rid of this information will do you a lot of good.

Clearing your physical clutter without resolving it can often be the cause of clutter in the mind. It is often a result of not having a To-Do list for your activities. A To-Do list will prioritize the activities you have for the day. Using a To-Do list will also show you in clear terms that you cannot complete all your tasks in one day. As a result, your mind will focus on the things that are currently of importance. Clutter will always be present in our daily lives. It may be in its digital or physical form when it appears. Although it is impossible to eliminate, there are always options to control clutter. Setting aside time for this process is necessary to increase your productivity level.

Chapter 8:
How to Set REAL Goals You Will Stick To

Creating goals is the first step to achieving success. Following through and achieving the goal is the most crucial part. It is also the most difficult. Learning some methods that can help in creating goals that you will follow is very important. Let us look at these rather simple methods

Create Goals from Your Vision

Having a vision is an integral part of creating a goal. There should also be a purpose behind any vision you have for your life. Once you are clear on these two aspects, it becomes easy to create a goal. At this stage, you may have multiple goals that you can develop from your vision. It is not a problem. Simply take time to write out these goals on paper, notebook, or journal. It should be a place that you can easily find it – some people prefer printing a Word document.

Visual aids are also useful when listing your goals. Creating goals requires commitment and seriousness. Goals that remain in an abstract form show that you are not willing to commit to these goals. Some key aspects to remember about creating goals include the following:

The Simple Yet Effective Methods to Cure Procrastination

- You should have both short-term and long-term goals.
- There should be a time-frame for achieving goals.
- Making it appear on paper makes it tangible.
- Be specific.
- Determine a means of measuring the goals.
- A goal should align with your passion. Aligning goals with passion makes it more exciting for you.

Start with Just One Goal

Trying to achieve too many things at once is an express route to failure. It is a common mistake that everyone makes. Although it is great you want to turn your life around, you can't make a long list of changes in one go.

To change a single aspect of your life, you require willpower. The amount of willpower will vary depending on what aspect of your life you intend to change. Too many aspects at once will need a ton of willpower which is why it is usually overwhelming. To put things in a way you can control, set a single achievable goal that you will focus on at a time. As you progress, you begin to get a handle on things. Later, you can add another goal.

Set SMART Goals

The SMART acronym is a rule that most people know about. Knowing in any context doesn't imply that it is being applied. Are you using the SMART principle in your daily life? If you want to set goals that are sure to achieve and which will also have a significant impact on your life, then it should be a SMART goal. Here is a breakdown of what the SMART acronym defines goals to be:

- Specific

- Measurable

- Achievable

- Relevant

- Time-bound

Setting Goals That Are Specific

A goal that is specific is well defined, clear, and easy to understand. It is not easy to identify your direction if your goal is generalized or vague. Your goals need to point in the direction you should take.

Having a specific destination will help in finding the right direction. A simple example will be setting a goal to build up your savings. You won't make any reasonable progress with a goal like 'save some money as soon as you get paid.' On the other hand, 'save $1,500 as soon as you get paid' will yield much better results.

Setting Goals That Are Measurable

A measurable goal is one that you can quickly assess for progress. It is a goal that includes amounts and dates with which you can make comparisons. Using our previous example, 'build-up savings' is a good goal but not a measurable goal. A measurable goal will be to 'build up my savings to $10,000 by the 1st of April.' With this goal, you can assess your progress on the 1st of March to see how much you have saved and how much to go.

Setting Goals That Are Achievable

Whatever goal you set should be a goal that you can achieve. Setting goals that are far beyond your reach will have negative impacts on you as an individual. Such goals will eat away at your confidence and work against your motivation. In the same regard, you may not get a reasonable sense of fulfillment if the goals you set are too easy to achieve. The low sense of fulfillment is because you don't need to put in a lot of effort. Your goals should be realistic and challenging.

Still working with our goal to build-up savings, a goal to 'save $1,500 as soon as you get paid' will be impossible if you make just $1,600. A more realistic and achievable goal will be to save the amount on a payment of $2,500. It is a more realistic goal which will come with lots of challenges. By setting this goal, you are telling yourself that you need to live with less than what you earn. If you find that you can survive on what is left, this goal can develop into a long-term strategy.

Setting Goals That Are Relevant

When setting a goal, ensure it is relevant to your development. It should be beneficial to your life or your career. As a result, it will be easier to focus on what you hope to achieve. When building up your savings, you can do so to register for a professional course. You may also do so to pay the college tuition for your child. Since these goals directly affect you, it becomes easy to focus on achieving them.

Setting Goals That Are Time-Bound

Adding a deadline to your goals is essential to measure your success. There is also a sense of urgency that you develop when you know you must meet a deadline. Just like in our example, our deadline was set to the 1st of April. If you can meet the target before this date, it will create room for celebration.

Set Short Term Milestones

Just because you set a single goal doesn't mean it will be straightforward to achieve. Sometimes, it becomes even simpler to procrastinate on these goals. A goal is usually a long-term destination. Having a short-term milestone is also important. A short-term milestone is an easy way to track your progress and manage your goal. You will be able to identify the progress you have made. It also provides opportunities to make changes when necessary. Create bite-sized pieces of your SMART goals and define actionable steps that will lead to achieving these goals.

The Simple Yet Effective Methods to Cure Procrastination

What Does Your Subconscious Mind Know About Your Goals?

A LOT OF PEOPLE often wonder why they fail to achieve their goals. It is easy to think that you will achieve a goal you have set due to the initial motivation that pushes you to set these goals. In truth, motivation doesn't last forever. Once the motivation fades away, interest in a goal quickly follows.

So how do you solve this problem?

The only solution is to burn your goal into your subconscious mind. By doing this, the actions you take become a habit. A habit is one of the most challenging things to break as an individual. Relying only on your motivation to achieve a goal will not yield the desired result you expect. Motivation is an excellent tool that you may be able to harness now but will be unavailable in the future. When you depend on habits, on the other hand, you can always leverage the positive influence.

- Create habits from your goals by programming them into your subconscious mind.

- Now, how do you burn your goals into your subconscious mind? Here are steps you can take to achieve this:

- Make sure you can see these goals every day by using a visual board.

- Regularly visualize a future where you have achieved your goals.

- Review your goals regularly.

- Repeat your goals daily to reaffirm these goals.

Inform Others about Your Goals

Your chances of success often become a lot higher when you share your goals with others. Your chances go up when you put your money on the line to achieve a goal. There are various people you can decide to tell about a goal you intend to achieve. It may be your boss, friend, or family. Once you tell someone else about your goal, it becomes more than just a dream. Anyone you tell will take it as their duty to monitor your progress. Try to give regular updates on your goal to anyone you tell about it.

Take Time to Review Your Goals

Just because you have a goal doesn't mean you are making any meaningful progress toward your goal. You may gradually be forgetting about these goals if you are not taking the right steps. You need to take the time to assess your progress.

If you fail to review your goals continuously, it is easy to get lost within the rush of your daily activities. It will shift your focus from the targets you have set to the targets directly in front of you. As a result, you will steadily forget about these personal targets. An easy way to maintain focus is to review the goal. By reviewing a goal, you will be able to get an insight into your progress and know if you are on a path that leads to your goal or one that deviates from the goal.

Do You Need Improvement?

As you make progress towards your goals, it is essential you also evolve your strategy. During the initial goal-setting phase, you will have come up with a plan as well as the actions to take in achieving a goal. It is also important you understand that things won't always go according to plan. Regardless of the setbacks you experience along the line; you need to keep pushing forward. Failures and mistakes are a huge part of the learning process.

Through your review, you will be able to understand the things that didn't work and why. The failures and mistakes translate to feedback. Learning from these feedbacks and making the necessary changes is the best way to reach your goals. Don't lose sight of your goals. Keep improving until you get a method that works effectively.

Chapter 9:
How to Stop Being Tired All the Time

If you feel you are tired all the time, there are a lot of other people with the same feeling. There are lots of individuals who struggle with the feeling of exhaustion all through the day. As a result, more individuals consume coffee and energy drinks to boost their mental alertness during the day. The real question – why do you always feel tired all the time?

Why Do You Feel Tired?

Various factors may result in a feeling of tiredness and fatigue. It doesn't matter if you are getting the recommended amount of sleep. If you still have no idea about the common causes of tiredness, here are some likely reasons why you feel this way:

Poor Quality Sleep

When determining the quality of your sleep, you need to check the amount of time you spend sleeping. Depending on your age, the recommended number of sleeping hours will vary. For adults, it is between seven – eight hours.

The Simple Yet Effective Methods to Cure Procrastination

If you assess your sleep duration and determine you are getting enough sleeping hours, then you should consult a doctor. A doctor can help determine if you are struggling with a medical condition that you don't know about. It is a common cause of poor quality of sleep. Various factors determine a high quality of sleep. These include the following:

- Waking up a maximum of once every night.

- The ability to fall asleep within thirty minutes.

- Spending a larger portion of your time on the bed asleep.

There are also external factors that may reduce the quality of your sleep. These include excess light in the room while sleeping, an irregular sleep routine, consuming alcohol or coffee before bed, leaving the TV on while sleeping, and other factors.

Stress

Irritation is a regular outcome of stress, but fatigue is also another common effect. In addition to causing fatigue, it also becomes difficult to get a good quality sleep when you are stressed out. Stressful situations may result from relationship issues, work pressure, or financial worries. There are lots of stressful situations you will have to face daily. There can be severe distortions to your sleep patterns when you are stressed. Since stress can result from worries, your worries may also be keeping you up all through the night.

When the body is under stress, chemicals like cortisol and adrenaline are produced. These are flight or fight chemicals. It is the process through which the body prepares for emergencies. As a result, the body subconsciously makes it harder to fall asleep when it is under stress.

Living on An Unhealthy Diet

The type of nutrients that you receive from your diet can affect the body. A diet that is unable to supply the necessary nutrients will lead to fatigue. It may include deficiency of vitamins and minerals like vitamin D, vitamin B12, iron, omega-3 fatty acids, and more. A low nutrient diet may result in the deficiencies of essential nutrients while you also may be losing energy when you follow a diet that is rich in added sugars and unhealthy fats. Consumption of processed foods may also add to the problem. The synthesis of sleep regulation neurotransmitters in the body requires these various minerals and vitamins. Consuming more vegetables and fruits can aid this process.

It is important you avoid junk food, candy, caffeine, and alcohol. The caffeine and alcohol can have adverse effects on your sleep pattern if taken before bed. The energy you get from junk foods, and candy only lasts for a short time which means the feeling of fatigue will return in a short time.

Dehydration

The Simple Yet Effective Methods to Cure Procrastination

A significant cause of dry-mouth and fatigue is dehydration. It is also important that you understand that dehydration isn't necessarily due to low water consumption. Vomiting, diarrhea, and excessive sweating can also lead to dehydration.

So, what is the simplest way to fight dehydration? Drink water to remain hydrated. It will also help to reduce the chances of sleepiness during the day time. Having a water bottle within an arm's length can help in this situation. In this case, water is the primary source to remain hydrated. Don't rely on alcohol. There is a fatigue-inducing and dehydrating effect that results from alcohol consumption. Other steps you can take include washing your face regularly, taking a shower regularly, and taking a glass of water before a meal.

A Sedentary Lifestyle

A common belief that we have is that sitting down will help to conserve our energy levels. Moving around is a more effective way to overcome fatigue. Spending too much time sedentary will deplete your energy much faster.

Having a proper balance between rest and activity is more beneficial. The body will also be more tired if you decide to perform excess physical activities. Nonetheless, exercising every day is important. When exercising or working out, you can aim for a single session of twenty minutes. It will be more beneficial than having multiple hours of gruesome workout. Please note working out in the evenings is not advisable. It will often make it more difficult for the body to fall asleep as you lay on the bed later at night.

A Medical Condition May Be the Problem

A lot of people attribute fatigue to their type of lifestyle. So, what happens when you make positive changes to your lifestyle without improvements? Then it is time to make an appointment with your doctor. There are various possibilities when considering medical conditions that lead to fatigue. Below are some of the common conditions that may be resulting in fatigue:

- Depression

- Sleep apnea

- Anemia

- Diabetes

- Thyroid disease

- Chronic Fatigue Syndrome

In some cases, certain medications may result in fatigue. It can be both an over-the-counter medication as well as a prescription medication.

How to Eliminate Exhaustion

The Simple Yet Effective Methods to Cure Procrastination

To assist in eliminating tiredness, you can use any of these strategies. The strategies listed are natural and work for the various causes.

Consistency in Your Sleep Routine

The consistency in this situation applies even on weekends. To eliminate fatigue, the most important first step is to improve the quality of your sleep. Follow the checklist below to encourage a high-quality sleep:

- You should have a bedtime that you follow both during workdays and on weekends.

- A combination of relaxing activities that form a bedtime ritual can be very helpful.

- Healthy habits like regular exercise, low caffeine consumption, no alcohol before bed, and avoiding tobacco can be beneficial.

- A room with a cold temperature without any lights or noise is essential to promote a good night's rest.

- Go outside and take a walk, visit your favorite park, and enjoy nature.

- Perform activities that reduce stress daily.

The duration of your sleep is also important. Getting less than seven hours of sleep at night may also lead to some health challenges such as:

- Depression.

- Mood, memory, and thinking impairment.

- Higher chances of heart problems and diabetes.

- Reduction in immunity.

Although the leading cause of exhaustion is a short duration of sleep, you may be risking certain health challenges if you are sleeping over nine hours every night. The challenges include headaches, obesity, and diabetes. Therefore, seven to eight hours of sleep is recommended for adults. Hitting the snooze button on your alarm may also be affecting your energy levels when you wake. The snooze time is often enough to doze off, but it is not enough to get restorative sleep. For this reason, it is better to avoid the snooze button.

Engage in Regular Physical Activities

Avoiding the temptation to lie on your couch when you are feeling tired is the best way to eliminate fatigue. Getting some exercise is your best option in this situation. Regularly performing physical activities can reduce fatigue and provide high levels of energy. It is also helpful in improving your mood and lowering anxiety. These are also other known causes of tiredness and fatigue. The physical activity you choose should be one you enjoy performing. The exercise also promote metabolism, and a twenty-minute jog can have significant benefits to the body.

Calm Your Mind

Some of the most significant energy drainers in the body are depression, negativity, and stress. Sometimes, seeking professional help may be the only way to rid all these negative feelings from your body. On the other hand, there are some more manageable steps you can take to free your mind from negative feelings and thoughts. You can start by meditating daily. There are lots of benefits you can gain from meditating for just five minutes every day. It can help improve your alertness and awareness while also calming the mind. Volunteering to help others is also another way to boost your energy levels and improve your mood. It also helps in making you feel good about yourself. Sometimes, we are often the cause of most of our problems. You may be harboring negative thoughts in the form of resentment, grudges, anger, or self-pity. Learning to let go of these emotions and forgive is one of the simplest ways to free your mind from the burden.

Another beneficial feeling that a lot of people tend to overlook is gratitude. Showing signs of gratitude and appreciating the things you have can help eliminate feelings of stress. Simply writing down all the things you are thankful for before going to bed can make you happy and remove negative thoughts that may keep you up all night.

Werner K. Clark

Find A Way to Deal with Stress

As an adult, it is common to deal with stress in one form or the other. Trying to address this stress is the only solution. When you are selecting a method to de-stress, it should be something consistent since your stress may also come up consistently. Taking a walk is one of the common ways to de-stress. You can take a walk around the neighborhood or walk up and down the stairs at work. It is also important you have a good view of your surroundings or an audio book that can take your mind away from the stressful thoughts. The release of endorphins is excellent for eliminating stress hormones.

Changing your view on a situation can also be very helpful. Create a positive outlook for a somewhat stressful situation. As an individual, you may find it stressful to take a longer route to work due to road construction. If you take it as more time for you to listen to a podcast, it can take the stress out of the process. Having fun is another method that is self-explanatory. There are different ways to have fun. What's more, a lot of them are free.

You can start by looking for activities that make you laugh. Laughter is one of the immediate cures for stress. You can get it by reading a comedy novel, watching funny movies, watching stand-up comedy, or simply listening to a friend that makes you laugh. There are other fun activities you can enjoy. Simply engaging in an activity that you are passionate about will provide a fun time. Trying out a new sport, visiting the new restaurant down the road, and making changes to your routine can also be very helpful.

Another easy way to unwind and relax is to be around plants. In a much broader perspective, being in tune with nature will help reduce stress and calm the brain. Taking a break during which, you can visit the local park or tend to your garden can help reduce any stress that has built up.

Eat Healthily

Your health is significantly influenced by the food we eat and those we avoid. The circadian rhythm of the body is also affected by the food we eat. For this reason, it is necessary to watch the food you consume. Making a few adjustments to the diet you consume can have a significant impact on the quality of your sleep. You can start by including cherries to your diet. It is an excellent natural source of melatonin. Melatonin is a hormone that is responsible for the control of the body clock. Staying away from alcohol is also important. All kinds of alcohol will have a negative impact on your sleep if consumed a short time before you go to bed.

Eating peanuts is also beneficial to individuals who find it hard to fall asleep. The peanuts promote the release of serotonin that makes us feel sleepy. Natural peanut butter will also produce the same effect. Another thing you can include in your diet is dark chocolate. It is a lot different from milk chocolate. Tyrosine is present in milk chocolate, and it functions as a stimulant by converting into dopamine. When starting your day, it is common for most people to avoid taking breakfast. Others may decide to load their stomach with lots of carbohydrates in the form of cereals, muffins, or donuts.

A large amount of carbohydrates will usually result in a rapid rise in blood sugar. As the blood sugar level returns to its normal level later in the day, you start craving junk food from the vending machine. Instead, it is important you add proteins to your meal to balance the carbohydrates. During breakfast, you can make scrambled eggs, take a protein bar, a protein-enriched smoothie, fruit with a bowl of yogurt, or simply spread peanut butter over your toast. By preventing rapid changes in blood sugar level, proteins can help keep you alert and awake.

Say No to Caffeine

CAFFEINE HAS BECOME an excellent option for individuals looking to mask their fatigue. It can provide a short-term energy boost, stimulate the nervous system, and make you feel awake. Nonetheless, various side effects come with the consumption of caffeine. They include the following:

- Insomnia

- Anxiety

- Abnormal or rapid heart rhythm

The Simple Yet Effective Methods to Cure Procrastination

- Dehydration
- Restlessness
- Dizziness
- Dependency
- Headaches

The dependency, in this case, is the need to consume more caffeine over time in order to maintain your alertness. The side effects that everyone will notice may differ from those of another individual. There are also many energy drinks and coffees that contain a large amount of sugar. These can lead to exhaustion at a much faster rate. Besides, the caffeine may also disrupt your standard body clock.

If you decide to stop your caffeine consumption, you can expect a few caffeine withdrawal symptoms. One such sign is an increase in drowsiness. In place of caffeine, you can choose to drink a lot of water all through the day. It is a natural way to make the body energized and alert. You should also eat foods like blueberries, oranges, spinach, almonds, and salmon that are energy-boosting foods.

Gain Vitamins from The Sun

Some essential nutrients assist in your fight against fatigue. Vitamin B and vitamin D are two such nutrients. It is also important to note that the sun can provide the body with these nutrients. A deficiency of vitamin D in the body is usually indicated by a feeling of moodiness, tiredness, or stress. If you spend just about fifteen minutes under natural light, you can help promote the production of these vitamins in the body. It can help maintain the energy levels of the body.

Take A Nap for An Energy Boost

The benefits of a nap are often understated. This short time of rest can produce improvements in memory, alertness, performance, and learning. The napping process also must be appropriately planned. A nap that exceeds twenty minutes can often have an adverse effect when you wake. Be sure to set an alarm before taking your nap. If you doubt the benefits of a power nap, then do you have a better answer to the reason why The Huffington Post and Google have designated zones for sleeping in the office?

Switch Off

Various devices like your television and smart phones usually have a significant effect on your sleep. In addition to leaving your smart phone on overnight, it is also possible that it doubles as your alarm clock. There have been conclusive results from research which show the effect of using your smart phone before bed. The bright light that emits usually tampers with your sleep patterns. It often makes it difficult to fall asleep. To avoid these situations, you should set a time at which you stop using these devices. You can then switch to a book or listen to music before bedtime. It is also important you get an alarm clock rather than using your smart phone for this function. It will also

The Simple Yet Effective Methods to Cure Procrastination

help prevent any interruption during sleep if you forget to disable an alarm at an earlier time.

Chapter 10:
The Secret to Work with Intense Focus

Focus is a valuable tool that determines how well you will be able to perform a task. If you lack focus, you will be giving in to distractions which will limit your ability to get work done. In our world of technology, a single click is all it takes to get to your distractions. Luckily, there are a few methods that can help in maintaining focus when you want to get work done. Some of these methods may require practice but offer massive rewards. Let's look at some of these methods below.

Work as an Individual

You may be aware of this to an extent, but you don't want to admit it. The people you work with are often the reason why you find it difficult to focus on the task at hand. Sometimes, it may not be intentional. When working with others, conversations may come up and you will want to be a part of these conversations. As the conversation progresses, you slowly lose focus on your task and turn your attention to the ongoing discussion. It is one of the reasons why some individuals tend to be less productive when their colleagues come over to their cubicle.

The Simple Yet Effective Methods to Cure Procrastination

In other cases, it is simply having someone working on another task that is different from yours which may affect your ability to maintain focus. It may be as a result of you visualizing what it will be like to perform the task the other person is currently working on. It may also simply be you taking an interest in the task to see how it ends. If you decide to work as an individual, you are separating yourself from others. When working far from other people, there is no opportunity to become a part of the conversation. It also improves your concentration on your task since there is no other person around whose task might seem more interesting. Working alone can also help you work with intense focus since you know you are the only one working on a task. You don't need to serve as a moderator to make other team members complete their part of the task.

Improve Your Focus by Taming Random Thoughts

Random thoughts are just that, random. These thoughts develop at an unexpected time within your head. It is a form of distraction that comes from within the body. It is commonly noticeable as the voice in your head speaking to you. It is an interruption that you are inevitably going to respond to if you don't have proper mental blocks. The following are some of the thoughts you may have:

- "Have I already sent the document?"

- "I do not remember locking my door before leaving home today."

- "Will I be able to get the loan from the bank?"

If these questions follow the same structure as those you usually have, then you need to learn how to curb these random thoughts. There are different methods you can use in curbing your random thoughts. These strategies are listed below:

- Use journals to write down thoughts.
- Use your breathing as a means of returning your focus to the task.
- Become adept at mindfulness.

Effectively Managing Stress

Developing a system that you can use in managing stress is vital if you hope to maintain focus. In your daily life, it is almost impossible to avoid stress. For this reason, you should prepare yourself to tackle this issue. Various activities help with stress reduction. Learning what activities work for your personality is also important. You should be considering activities like healthy eating, meditation, yoga, walking, running, etc.

Mindfulness

Another effective way to maintain focus is through mindfulness. This is a topic that should interest you at this moment. Mindfulness is a method of increasing your awareness of the task you are doing and where you are. When you practice mindfulness, it will make it possible for you to focus on the work that is directly in front of you. It also improves your concentration on a conversation or your ability to notice the environment when taking a walk. There are different ways to engage in mindfulness including the following:

- Mindful Movement such as Yoga.

- Meditation.

- Mindfulness-based stress reduction.

Being in the Present

A common reason why you may be losing focus is due to your worry about the future or reminiscence of the past. If you often get consumed by these thoughts, then it will be difficult to focus on the present. You are entirely out of sync with what is happening in the present.

Understanding that you cannot change the past and learning that you will never be able to predict the future is essential. You can only learn from the mistakes of the past and make changes to avoid a repeat of these mistakes. Taking full control of your thoughts and living in the present will provide a lot of benefits to your mental focus. You can remain sharp by paying attention to the task at hand. Most times, using your smart phone can often take your mind away from the present. You may find an old picture that brings back memories on your phone. It is why you need to clear all these distractions. Many other methods have been discussed in previous chapters. They include the following:

- Focusing on one task at a time.
- Eliminating potential distractions.
- Pre-committing to a task.
- Taking breaks.

Chapter 11:
Essential Apps that FORCE You to Be More Productive

Most of the apps that force you to commit to a task or goal are popularly known as commitment apps. These apps require you to make a commitment to achieve a goal. The commitment is necessary to prompt you into action. Some apps require commitments in the form of money you put on the line or your reputation. Others may limit your access to things you find enjoyable but unproductive. Below are some of the popular apps you should be using:

Beeminder
Beeminder is a platform that helps to keep you on track to achieving your goals. It creates a yellow brick road that you need to always remain on. The platform automatically creates the yellow brick road as soon as you input your goal. It allows users to input a goal that they want to achieve and quantify these goals. In a quantifiable term, you can add a data point (+1) every time you take a positive step towards your goal. Data points that fall on the yellow brick zone mean that you are safe and on the course. Any data point that doesn't fall on the yellow brick road indicates that you are off course. When a data point goes off course, you lose money.

Where Can I Use Beeminder?

The Beeminder website is available for use on your computer. For easy on-the-go access, you can also download the mobile app for Android and iOS devices. The apps allow users to view their dashboard that shows their progress, sends reminders, and inputs new data. To create a new goal, adjust your yellow brick road, or make any other significant changes, you need to use the Beeminder website.

Setting Up A Goal and The Types of Goals Available on Beeminder

To set up a new goal, all you need to do is to click on the 'New Goal.' As soon as you click on this button, the platform will require you to select the type of goal you want to set up. Below are the different types of goals you can set up on Beeminder:

Do More Goals

The Do More goals are the most common types of goals on the platform. As the name implies, it helps increase how much you perform an activity. Goals that fall within this category include jogging and studying more. It is not the same as a goal you would like to do more frequently.

Weight Loss Goals

What is the hint you get from the name of this goal? Yes, it is that simple. It is a goal that assists with your weight loss process. If you need to lose ten pounds in the next five weeks, you only need to set up this goal and input your results daily. Weigh yourself and input your current weight. There are also other types of goals including the following:

- Do fewer goals- it is a type of goal for activities you want to do at a reduced rate.

- Odometer goals – this is a goal that adds up over time like how you keep getting to a higher page when reading a book.

The two goals listed above require the Infinibee premium plan.

What Can You Find on Your Graph?

There is a graph that will be displayed on the goal page. Above the graph, you can find a derailment countdown while there is an input space below the graph. The things that you find on the graph include the following:

- Yellow Brick Road

- Road Dial

- Akrasia Horizon.

How Do You Input Data on The Platform?

There are different options for data input on Beeminder. It can simply be using the data entry box that is below the graph. Other methods include sending a response to the bot emails, through text message, or using the mobile app. There is a specific format for inputting data on the platform.

Reminders

The reminders from Beeminder come in on emergency days. The default time to receive a reminder is around 9:30 am on these days. If the time is not convenient, you can change it in the goal settings menu. If you don't take any action, you will continue receiving these reminders at a higher frequency. Zeno polling – that is how Beeminder describes the reminders. It is also possible to turn it off when necessary.

Derailing

Derailing on this platform implies that there is a data point that doesn't fall on the yellow brick road. In this case, the data point will appear in the color red. It is what creates an emergency day. If at the end of the day you are unable to get the data point back on the yellow brick road, it leads to a derailment. The deadline for a derailment can be customized in the settings menu. To eliminate difficulty trying to catch-up after a derailment, the road adjusts to the current data point.

What are Legit Checks?

A legit check is an email that you receive from the platform any time you derail. Through the email, the platform will try to find out if you have derailed from your yellow brick road or you have simply failed

The Simple Yet Effective Methods to Cure Procrastination

to input the latest data. It is how the platform avoids making erroneous deductions. It is also more comfortable than having to refund money after deductions. If you feel this is just an easy way out of your commitments, then you can use the 'Weaselproof Me' option in the goal settings menu. By checking this option, you may need to send additional proof that it wasn't a legitimate derailment.

Pledges

Beeminder usually requires users to enter a credit card detail. The charges for your derailment are deducted from the credit card. You can start using the platform without a credit card. In this case, your first derailment will cause the platform to freeze your goal. At this point, there is no money on the line so no consequence for your derailment. To continue with your goal, it will be necessary to make a pledge at this point. The pledge is usually $5 that will be charged on the next derailment.

The charge for derailment increases as the number of derailments increases. It follows a progression that looks like, $5, $10, $30, $90, $270, $810. The charge will keep increasing until it reaches an amount you are not willing to lose. At this point, you will have the right motivation.

The Most Dangerous Writing App

It is a web app that is designed to prompt you to write by pushing you to your limits. As a writer, it is common to experience writer's block.

It may be due to your fears of not being good or the inability to face criticism from your readers. Whatever the reason, it is crucial you find a way to overcome this problem. That is where the Most Dangerous Writing app is helpful.

How does this app push you to the limit? Simple – it deletes any progress you have made if you remain inactive for an extended period. To start using the app, you will need to start a session. The session can be as short as five minutes and can also span multiple hours. You must keep writing for as long as the session is active to avoid losing your progress. When it is about to delete your progress, there will be a countdown warning. You may not consider it as a serious writing app, but it can be an excellent way to eliminate feelings of self-doubt when writing. By blurring everything you have written you don't have the opportunity to over-analyze. It forces you to come up with new ideas.

Freedom

An essential app that helps in blocking distractions is Freedom. The app is excellent for preventing access to websites and sites that may distract you from important activities that you need to focus on. It is suitable for use on iPhone, iPad, or computer.

Freedom allows users to create a session and then select the things they would like to block. It may be your access to Facebook, Twitter, or the internet. The session may also be recurring for a specific period every day of the week. If you find it easy to get distracted even during a session, you can also use a Locked Mode. In this mode, it becomes impossible to change the settings of the app while a session is in progress.

Stickk

Stickk is a platform that assists you in achieving any goal you have set. It promotes your productivity by making you place something of value on the line. The consequence of failing to reach your goal is the loss of whatever you put on the line. You can decide to put money of reasonable value on the line or stake your reputation. If you fail to reach a goal, you will lose the money you have put on the line. In the same regard, if you decide to stake your reputation, the platform will notify your family and friends anytime you fail to achieve a goal. As a result, you slowly damage your reputation. By holding you accountable, the platform prompts you to act. The success of the platform is noticeable in the way it makes users commit to a goal.

The unique feature on the platform is how it forces you to pay up for your failure. Since you put the money on the line before making the commitment, there is no opportunity to go back on your goals. It is also sure that you will lose the money if you fail since it is not your family or friend that you can easily convince to refund the money.

A Brief Example on the Use of Stickk

A simple goal that you may want to achieve is building your savings up to $10,000 in the next ten weeks. This is a large goal, and the first step to take is to break it down into smaller parts (a simple strategy from lessons within this book). A breakdown of this goal will be to save $1,000 every week.

On the Stickk platform, there is a Commitment Contract available. To complete this contract, you can type in your goal to save $1,000 per week for the next ten weeks. You can then fund the Stickk escrow account with an amount that will be painful to lose. It can be $500 in this case. To ensure you don't lose your money, you will keep updating your progress every week. If you are unable to meet your $1,000 target for a week, you will lose $50. A lot of people may be wondering how Stickk will be able to determine if you are making progress. The platform usually allows users to add a referee. A referee is a person who will track your progress to determine if you are telling the truth or not. The site also uses the honor system.

You may be considering the design of the platform as a scheme to get rich by the developers. Why? Well, where is my money going? To avoid these issues, Stickk allows users to select an organization that gets the money you lose. It refers to these organizations as 'anti-charities.' The reason for this unique name is that any charity you select will be one that you don't like at all. As a way to prompt you to action, the platform makes donations to the cause that you don't believe in. Some of the anti-charities on the platform include:

The Simple Yet Effective Methods to Cure Procrastination

- NRA Foundation
- William Jefferson Clinton Presidential Library
- Educational Fund to Stop Gun Violence
- Americans United for Life
- Nature Conservancy
- George W. Bush Presidential Library
- NARAL Pro-Choice America Foundation.
- The option to pick a friend or random charity is also available.

Will It Work?

The reason why a lot of people give up on their goals is the lack of consequences for their actions. The lack of accountability also supports this behavior. You can use Stickk as a tool to prompt you into action.

RescueTime

RescueTime is a tracking application that is useful for recording the time spent visiting a site or using a specific program. It makes it possible for you to identify how you spend each minute of your day. Using the application, you will be able to identify areas where you are spending more time than necessary. Setting up the application for use is also easy. You may require about a week to tweak the system, but once it is complete, you are all set to boost your productivity.

Setting Up RescueTime

The first step is to install the program on your computer. It will be the only useful step you will be able to take for a while. Since you will need at least two days' worth of data, you will need to wait a bit to reorganize how you use your time. To get the installer, visit the RescueTime website. On the site, you will find a 'Get Started' button that you need to click. It then comes with the option to select an account type. There is a free account and a pro account available. Selecting the free account should offer the things you need to utilize your time efficiently. On the pro account, you get features like individual documents tracking within a program, website blocking, and alerts. It is possible to get some of these features by using other apps like Freedom for site blocking. You also get a fourteen-day trial during which you can test the unique features of the pro account to decide if it is worth getting.

You will need to create a username and password after selecting the account type. There will be a prompt to download the installer. During the installation, the wizard will require you to input activities that you consider as 'distractive' or 'productive.' You also have an option to skip this selection process. Now, you can install RescueTime on your computer and then run the program. It will run in the background until you decide to shut it off. It also has a pause option which can be for fifteen minutes, sixty minutes or pause till the next day.

Running the program may not be a suitable option for you. In this case, you can right-click on the icon to open a menu with the 'Dashboard' option available. On the dashboard, the right-hand corner has a settings link through which you can access the 'Monitoring' tab on the program. The 'Monitoring' tab allows you to choose the days and the time during which you want the program to run. It is better to make these settings on the days and times during which you work. There are other settings you can also adjust. After saving the settings, you need to let the program run for a few days to gather the necessary data.

How Long Should You Let It Run?

After running the program for two days, you can decide to make changes based on the data it has accumulated. The main question here is; is it an accurate reflection of your week? There will be days when your schedule is not as tight as other days. If you are only using data from two days out of a five-day work week, you will still need to make changes later. Instead, you can choose to wait about a week before heading to the RescueTime Dashboard to make the necessary changes. As a result, you won't need to return anytime soon to tweak the settings.

Analyzing the Data

Since you have been able to accumulate a reasonable amount of data, it is now time to analyze the data. On the RescueTime Dashboard, you will find charts and graphs that can tell you about your time usage during the week. On the right side of the screen, you will find tabs such as the 'Time Reports' tab. By clicking on this tab, it will provide access to graphs which are more detailed. The graphs available include:

The Overview Tab

Here, you will find a graph which shows your activities by grouping them into communication and entertainment activities. There is a color-coding on the graph with the red indicating an activity that is distracting while a blue color indicates productive activities.

Activities

The activities page displays the sites you visit and the programs you make use of on your computer. The time you spend on these programs or sites is also available in this section. Your productivity level is also indicated using the color-coding method.

Categories

The Categories tab is a more in-depth graph that splits your activities further into categories such as Calendars, Meetings, Social Networking, and News/Opinion.

Goals

The Simple Yet Effective Methods to Cure Procrastination

What do you want to achieve? What can this application help you change? In the goals section, you can easily set goals within the application. It can be a simple goal or a more complex one depending on the changes you hope to achieve.

Efficiency

The Efficiency section contains a chart with just one bar. The bar indicates your percentage efficiency. It is the time spent on productive activities in a percentage. Sometimes, the efficiency may not be as useful as the information you get from the Activities section. The period for each graph can be adjusted to display reports in respect to day, week, month, or year depending on your preference.

Adjusting How the Application Categorizes Your Activities

There is also a 'Categorize Activities' link on the Activities screen that is more useful than you can imagine. Using social media sites will often be labeled as being a distraction if no-one knows your reason for visiting these sites. The same also applies to how RescueTime categorizes certain activities. In some cases, Instant Messaging may be labeled as a distracting activity. In truth, you may need it to communicate with colleagues during work periods. In the context of the job you are performing, it is an incorrect analysis. The 'Categorize Activities' page enables you to adjust such descriptions. Plus, and minus signs are present on the right side of a row which allows you to change the productivity level of activity.

Sometimes, when adjusting the productivity level of an activity, it may also be necessary to change the category. It is often due to the inability of RescueTime to deduce the function of an application. The option of changing the label of an entire category is also available from the settings. A lot of people need this useful feature if they require social networking sites to work. Since the default label is 'Distracting,' it is possible to change all social networking sites to 'Productive.'

It can either be by changing the productivity level of an entire category or simply creating a new category. The changes you make in the settings will reflect on your graphs instantly. Slowly and steadily, the graph will be becoming an excellent reflection of your daily activities. It will give better pointers to your productivity level, how you are spending time, and the various weaknesses you are struggling with. It is important to know what causes the most distraction during your work periods. Once you can take note of it, you will be motivated to avoid using the program or visiting the site.

Review Regularly

Regular review of the application is the only way to get the best results. Review of the application will become the next course of action as soon as you begin to get accurate results from your graphs. The review of the application should be about once or twice a week. Sometimes, at the end of a very unproductive day, it will be very beneficial to visit your dashboard. It can identify areas where you lost track of your essential tasks. Minimizing distracting activities is important

The Simple Yet Effective Methods to Cure Procrastination

when reviewing. It is essential you avoid eliminating such activities totally as it is often necessary to take breaks to replenish your energy levels. Nonetheless, if you find out that you are spending the most time on Facebook or Twitter, then you will need to cut back on time spent.

Chapter 12:
Wake Up Motivated Every Day Hack

Throughout this book, we have been discussing some of the most critical aspects of procrastination and how it can affect your life. Understanding how it differs from laziness has also been a real eye-opener. Time-wasting is one of the most significant causes of procrastination in life. Learning how to avoid this dream killer will also result in massive rewards as soon as you put what you have learned into action.

You schedule is not going to be as desirable as you want it to be. Some days, it can be so tight you have only a little time to take a break. Nonetheless, there is a valuable insight into how you can use technology to get the best results from a hectic schedule. If you think there is no powerful tool to motivate yourself intrinsically, I'm sure you have realized your error. Willpower is a tool no-one teaches you how to harness in school. It is something you must develop on your own. Learning to make the most of this vital tool is the key to success in achieving your goals.

Developing sticky habits is something we often overlook. We often misplace our priorities by performing an activity for short term

The Simple Yet Effective Methods to Cure Procrastination

rewards rather than long term benefits. Habits that stick usually require a different approach with a focus on the long-term benefits that I have thoroughly explained within this book.

If you bought this eBook looking to reinforce your belief that procrastination is the only killer of your productivity, you should have realized your mistake at this point. There are subtle productivity killers that you are indulging daily. It is time to have a re-think and perform a complete check to determine where you are going wrong.

Tiredness is often the result of trying to achieve more in the day at the expense of your sleep. Other various factors may lead to this undesirable event. If you have been paying attention to the tips within this eBook, you should be noticing significant improvements in how you feel when you wake up. Focusing solely on the task at hand can be quite difficult. There are some traditional methods that I have put into this eBook, but I have taken a step further to tell you the best way to utilize technology. Using the various commitment apps, I have described earlier, you will not only be improving your focus but also your productivity.

My Final Words

As my reward to you for getting this far, I will be giving you a tip you can apply to automatically motivate yourself to work as soon as you wake up. The first step is to develop a cue that serves as a trigger for your habits. It is also possible for a cue to trigger a mindset in you. It is the crucial quality I want you to remember.

Every time you get new shoes from your favorite designer, you always become more confident when walking around the streets. You haven't particularly done anything spectacular – except changing the shoes on your feet. It is you associating the new shoes to your confidence. Wearing new shoes is your way of gaining a confidence boost for the day. It blocks out all the negative comments that would pull you down on any other day. It is a cue that puts you in the right mindset.

Having new shoes as your cue is not a great choice. Find something that is easy to repeat daily. It can be shaving every day or tying your hair in a ponytail. A common cue with most individuals who work in an office is wearing a tie on a shirt. Once they dress this way, their mindset automatically switches to the hard work ahead.

The Simple Yet Effective Methods to Cure Procrastination

Different things might serve as your cue. These are things you do on the days you achieve a lot. Finding the unique thing you do on such days will help determine your cue. Remember, it might be a simple, insignificant activity like making your bed before leaving. In addition to motivation, using a cue will also result in more willpower.

If you find this book helpful in anyway a review to support my endeavors is much appreciated.

Werner K. Clark

The Simple Yet Effective Methods to Cure Procrastination

www.ingramcontent.com/pod-product-compliance
Lightning Source LLC
Chambersburg PA
CBHW060611080526
44585CB00013B/779